Musical Theater Voice Pedagogy: The Art and Science

by

Christopher Arneson, DMA

&

Kirsten S. Brown, EdD

Musical Theater Voice Pedagogy: The Art And Science

by

Christopher Arneson, DMA

Kirsten Shippert Brown, EdD

Anatomical portions of this text include stock images from Adobe, used under license. Additional images from the Netter Collection are used under license and by permission of Elsevier. Images related to acoustics and resonance first appeared in *Your Voice: An Inside View 3* (McCoy, 2020) and are used with permission of the author and publisher.

ISBN: 978-1-7335060-5-2

Inside View Press
Gahanna, Ohio

www.voxped.com

Printed in the United States of America

Edited by Scott McCoy

Table of Contents

Acknowledgements

We were acutely aware throughout this endeavor that we owe much of our expertise to our predecessors, teachers, colleagues, and friends. We stand on the shoulders of giants, and are so grateful to each of you, particularly those whose work we've cited throughout this book.

We owe great thanks to our editor, colleague, and friend Eva Tamsky. Her work was invaluable in creating a resource that is clear, practical, and useful. Many thanks also to Ulyana Patoka at upillustrations@gmail.com for our cover art, and to Felicia Betts for her assistance in preparing the final draft.

Thanks also to our colleague, editor, and publisher Scott McCoy for the use of many illustrations from his book, *Your Voice: An Inside View*.

To our students, with whom our ideas have been tested and refined: thank you for sharing your voices and selves with us. Much of what we've written in this book we learned from you.
– C.A. and K.S.B.

Thanks to:
James Lipton, Nova Thomas and Keith Buhl, my collaborators at the Actor's Studio Drama School where we developed and implemented a curriculum which became the foundation of all my work in professional voice training.
– C.A.

To my husband, Dan: Your support and encouragement make all my work possible. I promise I'll wait at least a week before starting another book.
– K.S.B.

Introduction

The Purpose of this Book

We often joke with our students that singing is the art of multitasking. In an effective performance, a singer is managing so many different processes simultaneously. They are positioning their bodies, controlling their breathing, coordinating their phonation, managing their support, choosing their registration, maintaining their resonance, and adjusting their articulation. They're following the contour of the melody and feeling the flow of the rhythm. They're remembering the words and the intention with which those words were written; they're inhabiting the character they're playing and living in that emotional world—and that's just the basics! Sometimes they're also watching a conductor, dancing, harmonizing with a cast member, or fussing with an unruly costume.

Singing, particularly in the musical theater genre, is not a single skill, but a vast and varied collection of competencies. Teaching someone to sing, therefore, means facilitating many kinds of learning. For instance, there is the scientific study necessitated by using an instrument housed within the human body. There's the analytical study of learning not only to read, but also to interpret sheet music. There's the literary and dramatic study of uncovering depth and meaning from words on a page. There's the physical work of acquiring incredibly fine motor control over muscles the student can neither feel nor see. Finally, there's the emotional learning that enables the singer to share their voice, in all their vulnerabilities, with an audience. Guiding a student through each of these minefields simultaneously is a daunting task.

We wish we could give you a perfect roadmap—a foolproof curriculum that guarantees success for all. But what makes singing magical is also what makes that impossible: its individuality. Every voice is part of a different human body, produced by a different human consciousness, shaped and molded by an entirely different set of experiences. That means every voice has the potential to say something different: to bring something novel and beautiful to our world. It also means no two paths begin or end in the same place.

Acting as a guide through each individual student's vocal, musical, and artistic wilderness means that voice teaching relies heavily on your ability to make effective choices about where to go next. This book is predicated on the idea that those choices must consider three factors:

1. The science and general function of the human voice,
2. The stylistic conventions of the music at hand, and
3. The talents, personality, and creativity of each student.

The purpose of this book is to explore musical theater vocal pedagogy in a way that integrates these factors. What we've provided is not a map, but a field guide: a tool that can strengthen your ability to make effective decisions as you and your student chart their wilderness together. We hope you'll walk away with tools to understand the landscape, and confidence in your ability to choose the right steps forward.

How to Read this Book

The first three chapters of this book serve as prerequisites for the following chapters and will explore a broad approach to the three key factors listed above. Chapters 4-10 are each devoted to a specific area of vocal technique. They will detail the anatomy and physiology applicable to that area of technique, how that area of technique is manipulated for the various styles of musical theater, and effective teaching strategies. Chapters 5-10 will also include a look back on the chapters that came before to integrate your understanding. The final chapter includes ideas that are vital to voice teaching that go beyond the topics in the rest of the book.

There are plenty of books and resources that are excellent sources of vocalises. While there are a few example exercises in each chapter, providing an exhaustive list of vocalises was not our goal. Rather, the vocalises in each chapter function as illustrations of the principles we've outlined and serve to demonstrate the kind of exercises you might choose based on your knowledge of the science, style, and student in front of you.

Who This Book is For

If you have students singing on Broadway, we're very flattered that you've picked up our book, but it wasn't meant for you. Our goal was to write for voice teachers who are looking to expand their knowledge and skills in their work with beginning and intermediate musical theater singers. Perhaps you're a young singer, just starting your career in voice teaching. Maybe you've been teaching classical singing for many years, and you're looking to apply your experience to this genre. Maybe you're a music educator who finds themselves coaching singers for the school musical. Or maybe you're a stellar musical theater singer, looking to make the bridge from performing to teaching. These are the people for whom we wrote this book. But whoever you are, we hope you find something useful to you here.

Chapter 1: The Science

Both authors of this book loathed studying science all through school. When you choose a career in the arts, you don't imagine that things like Boyle's law or the Bernoulli effect (we'll define these concepts in later chapters) will become part of your daily life—maybe you chose a career in the arts specifically to avoid such things! You may not view yourself as someone who works with, in, and around science. But, ultimately, you are someone who works with the human body and helps others understand how to use it. We encourage you to embrace the duality of your role as a voice teacher as you toggle, and even blur the lines, between science and art. This world of scientific knowledge is as open to you as you would like.

Why Science: Adaptability and Agency

Many successful voice teachers rarely integrate voice science into their teaching. Some argue that a cognitive understanding of the voice doesn't translate into the ability to use it more effectively. Others see voice science as superfluous and over-complicated; after all, people have been singing and learning to sing for millennia, long before voice science became a topic of study. But if your reference point for your teaching is not the physiological function of the voice, then it must be the methods and strategies you have learned through your own study and from other voice teachers. There is, of course, wisdom in these sources, but relying on them solely leaves you less able to adapt to new situations, new vocal or musical styles, and new students.

Particularly in the musical theater and contemporary commercial genres, styles are constantly changing. The rate of change makes it difficult for voice teachers to keep up; indeed, within 20 years, much of what we've written here about styles could be obsolete. But human evolution happens much more slowly, and the larynx, the diaphragm, and the vocal tract will still be the same. Understanding voice science means that learning to teach new styles or genres is a matter of connecting its sounds and conventions to what you already know about vocal function, rather than learning a whole new set of exercises, language, and ideas. Similarly, when you encounter a student for whom your habitual methods aren't effective, you can adapt by selecting, or even designing, exercises that encourage the same function but cater to their needs. With this knowledge, you can respond to whatever you hear in the moment with flexibility and fluidity.

Many voice teachers who rely on voice science in this way still choose not to share this knowledge with their students. It's true that few students come to our studios expressly looking for a science lesson, but what they are often seeking is greater control over their instrument. We argue that at least basic knowledge of how that instrument functions is essential to gain a sense of agency: the feeling that you have control over your actions and their consequences. In our experience, students don't always need to know the finer points of anatomy and physiology or the laws of acoustics to experience this benefit; simple explanations work well, especially in the beginning of study and for younger students. Complex terminology isn't essential either: you could say "stretching muscles" instead of cricothyroid or "resonances" instead of formants. When information about the function of the voice is shared with singers with appropriate depth, and in a way that is integrated with their experiences of their voice, we find they are hungry for that information and use it to become more independent singers.

Giving your students an understanding of the physiology of the voice also allows them to sort through the copious amounts of information about singing that come to them from other teachers, other singers, books, and even social media. Voice science can be their north star and keep them from going adrift when you're not there to guide them. We encourage all voice teachers to empower their students with this knowledge.

The Flowchart

The middle chapters of this book are organized according to what we call *The Flowchart*. The Flowchart is a linear conception of the physiological process of singing; it came about as an attempt to organize the many moving parts of the singing process, specifically for students of voice pedagogy. We find it's a useful way not only to break up the science into meaningful chunks, but also to categorize areas of vocal competence, exercises, and even repertoire.

Alignment > Breathing > Phonation > Support > Registration > Resonance > Articulation

Each stage—and each of chapters 4 through 10—represents a specific part of the vocal process, as defined by specific anatomical structures and physiological functions. They follow the order of an ideal vocal process, beginning with alignment. We use the term "alignment" to refer to the way a singer positions their body for singing. Muscles and structures outside the vocal tract come into play here, like the hips, knees, and ankles. But we also use this section of the book (Chapter 4) to describe the anatomy of the vocal tract and how it is intricately connected to the rest of our bodies.

The second area is breathing, which, for our purposes, refers exclusively to inhalation (exhalation and breath control is an area unto itself). Inhalation is technically the beginning of the singing process, but we chose to place it after alignment because of the ways in which an efficient breath relies on solid alignment (more on that in Chapter 5). This section is where we discuss the role of the diaphragm, the lungs, and exactly how the process of bringing air into our bodies works.

Following breathing is phonation. Phonation broadly refers to the process of making any vocal sound, but here we use that term to address the anatomy of our larynx and vocal folds, the muscles that bring them together and pull them apart, and the forces that initiate and maintain vocal fold vibration. This chapter—Chapter 6—will discuss onsets, vibrato, and issues like breathiness or a pressed sound.

Chapter 7 is about support. We use the term support to refer to exhalation, and more specifically, the way we manage that exhalation for singing. We'll talk about the abdominal muscles, the rib cage, and the reasons why the vocal folds themselves are an integral part of this process (which is why support follows phonation).

Registration comes next. Scientifically, this means we'll focus on the muscles that manipulate the length and tension of our vocal folds, laryngeal position, and the ways in which these adjustments change what we hear. We'll also discuss the ways in which vocal fold length, tension, and laryngeal position affect the other parts of the singing process.

Most of these sections deal with anatomy and physiology, but resonance deals with the science of acoustics. In Chapter 9, we'll talk about how the shape of our vocal tract changes our sound to create different vowels and timbres. You'll encounter topics like formants, vowel modification, and nasality.

Finally, Chapter 10 deals with articulation, or more specifically, the muscles and structures we use to form consonant sounds. We'll explore all the ways the jaw, tongue, soft palate, and muscles of the face can affect the voice—for good and bad!

We find that this order of events is helpful for people in learning how the voice functions and how to aid that function. But it might not be the right sequence for all students as they learn how to manipulate that function within their own bodies. As we'll discuss further in this chapter and future chapters, the whole vocal mechanism is incredibly interconnected, so any one entry point can lead to the others. And different students might have an easier time finding their way from different starting points. As we mentioned in the introduction, there is no single right way to teach someone how to sing.

Interactivity

> *In the old linear view, the voice was like squeezing the bulb on the horn of an old Model T Ford—a simple case of one cause, one effect... Instead, beautiful singing should be seen more like shaking a bush—when one of the branches is moved, all the others are affected. – Clayne Robison*[1]

Suggesting that vocal function is entirely linear is inaccurate; in truth, all the parts of the voice are connected in more of a web than a straight line. Articulation affects support; resonance affects breathing; registration affects alignment. Every part of the voice is interconnected.

What is linear, however, is a book; the format of this project dictates that we impose an order. But, to aid you in making non-linear connections, each of Chapters 5 through 10 will end with a section detailing that area's influence on and interaction with the areas that have come before. We hope you'll think of the Flowchart not as a perfectly encapsulated model of vocal function, but as one path through the web—because

---

[1] Clayne Robison. *Beautiful Singing*. Xpressions, 2001: 119-120,

voice instruction is more effective when teachers start listening and students start singing with the implications of this interactivity in mind.

Gender and Voice Terminology

You'll notice as you move through this book that we eschew terms like "women's voices" or "the male voice." These gendered terms are exclusionary and, for so many trans and nonbinary singers, simply inaccurate. The idea that gender is limited to a binary is both flawed and harmful, so we will not perpetuate it here.

Unfortunately, most if not all musical theater repertoire still operates under this binary, and the repertoire makes different demands of men and women. Also, the sex hormones, testosterone and estrogen, affect the voice, meaning that there are anatomical differences between voices that are more influenced by testosterone and those more exposed to estrogen. It's difficult to eliminate the idea of a binary entirely, but we can at least disconnect our associations of voice type from gender. We choose to use the term *treble voices* to describe those voices that sing mostly in the range of the treble clef, and *modal voices* to describe those voices that sing mostly in the range of the bass clef. This solution is more of a stopgap than a permanent fix, but a truly inclusive approach to singing, voice teaching, and musical theater will only come as the result of many smaller shifts across the theater industry, academia, and in voice studios like yours. We want our writing to be a part of that shift, and we hope your teaching will be as well.

Chapter 2: The Art

Here we come to a completely new genre—the musical play as distinguished from musical comedy. Now ... the play was the thing, and everything else was subservient to that play. Now ... came complete integration of song, humor, and production numbers into a single and inextricable artistic entity. – The Complete Book of Light Opera[2]

The first "complete integration of song, humor, and production numbers," the above quote is referencing, was *Showboat*. While *Showboat,* which premiered in late 1927, wasn't the first musical, it was the genesis of many defining traits of the modern musical theater genre, and the first book musical. Musical theater is, as we will continue to emphasize throughout this book, primarily about the words and the drama, while music, dance, and production design serve to bolster the story. The classical and pop genres prize the music and/or the aesthetic above all else, but musical theater is fundamentally *theater*, and the story is always the most important thing. This true integration of story and music is what makes a musical so powerful; we connect emotionally with the narrative, which the music heightens. In this chapter, we provide a brief study of the genre, not to box your students into strict conventions, but to further their understanding of the power of musical theater and enhance their ability to wield it.

Commonalities in Musical Theater Repertoire

Most of this chapter is devoted to the ways in which the music of the musical theater genre is varied. But there are some commonalities in the musical theater song repertoire that, generally, persist across style and era. You could spend a lifetime discovering the specific conventions and techniques of every pocket of the musical theater genre, but fortunately, there are some unifying elements that give us, and our students, a way in.

The first of these is the connection between the music and the character. Unlike many pop songs that express one relatable idea, or an art song that takes its text from a stand-alone poem, the best musical theater songs are deeply connected to the

---

[2]Lubbock, Mark, and David Ewen. *The Complete Book of Light Opera*. Appleton-Century-Crofts, 1963: 753.

character who sings them. The convention of the "I want" song is a great example. Many musicals begin with a song from the main character that expresses what they want, like "Wouldn't it be loverly" from *My Fair Lady*, or "Waving through a window" from *Dear Evan Hansen*. These songs are unique and specific to the character that sings them, are vehicles of the plot, and imbue the audience with a sense of purpose and anticipation. Who the character is and the story that surrounds them should always be a fundamental part of preparing any musical theater repertoire.

Musical theater songs are also united by big emotions—after all, something must motivate these characters to break into song! Those big emotions can come in response to anything, like a life-changing assignment in Africa, as in "You and me (but mostly me)" from *The Book of Mormon*, or a simple shampoo as in "I'm gonna wash that man right out of my hair" from *South Pacific*. Sometimes these songs demand over-the-top performances, while others are more grounded in realism. But they always demand vulnerability and commitment from singers, and a willingness to make bold choices.

Finally, the genre is united by the authentic and organic style of communication that comes from speech. This principle is as true in the musicals of Rodgers and Hammerstein as it is in *Hamilton*, and it can provide an easy jumping off point in our teaching. Grounding your student's practice and performance in coordinated, flexible, and efficient speech provides an easy bridge between the function of their singing voices and the way we naturally communicate.

Different Eras and Styles of Musical Theater

Every period and style of musical theater has its own set of conventions that demand specific vocal colors and textures. Nasal twang, borrowed from the country music genre, is an obvious example, as is the operatic "legit" sound found in earlier musicals. A big part of musical theater singing training is working toward versatility and fluency across styles. Singers should experiment with a wide variety of vocal qualities to become as flexible and fluid in their vocal use as possible. Jazz, Blues, Rock, Pop,

Country, Gospel, Operetta, Latin—all of these musical genres can be found in Musical Theater![3]

Early Musicals and Influences: pre-1940

The musical, like jazz, is a quintessentially American art form, and has been forged from many influences: comic opera, operetta, English music hall, minstrel shows[4], vaudeville, and others. European composers certainly influenced the music in musicals, but the distinctively American sound is attributable to Stephen Foster (1826-1864) and his songs, like "Oh! Susanna," "Camptown Races" and "Old Folks at Home (Swanee River)." As we mentioned at the top of this chapter, *Showboat* was not the first musical; that honor belongs to *The Black Crook*, which premiered in 1866. Nearly forty years later, the man who came to be recognized as the grandfather of the American musical comedy, George M. Cohan (1878-1942), wrote *Little Johnny Jones* (1904), which included the first tribute to this new art form, "Give my regards to Broadway."

Jerome Kern began his career in the same year, as his songs were inserted into shows whose scores were written mostly by other composers, as was the convention of early musicals both on Broadway and in London. Kern went on to write the music for *Showboat*, in collaboration with lyricist Oscar Hammerstein. This era also produced enduring shows by prominent composers like Cole Porter, Rodgers and Hart, Irving Berlin, and the Gershwin brothers. George Gershwin, more than any other composer, introduced the language of jazz to Broadway.

The influence of jazz also affected singing in this era. Ethel Merman rose to fame during what is often called "The Jazz Age," and she became a benchmark for the Broadway sound. The sound was bright and brassy, with lots of twang, and sometimes utilized full chest voice. Vibrato was still used but delayed to the end of the note after a period of straight tone. Because these were musical comedies, the diction was

---

[3] For a comprehensive discussion of the various styles in musical theater see *Acting in Musical Theater: A comprehensive Course*. Joe Deer and Rocco Dal Vera. Routledge, 2021.

[4] Minstrel shows were an inherently racist form of entertainment, popular in America from the 1830's to the early 1900's. Their defining feature was white actors dressed in blackface, performing songs and comedy skits based on black stereotypes.

Vicky Gan. "The Story Behind the Failed Minstrel Show at the 1964 World's Fair." Smithsonian Magazine. April 28, 2014.

https://www.smithsonianmag.com/history/minstrel-show-1964-worlds-fair-180951239/

paramount, but often done in a New York accent. Important shows from this era include *The Boys from Syracuse* (1938), *The Cradle will Rock* (1938), *Babes in Arms* (1937) and *Anything Goes* (1934).

Golden Age Musicals: 1940s – Early 1960s

The Broadway musical evolved dramatically when Richard Rodgers and Oscar Hammerstein forged a new collaboration, beginning with *Oklahoma!* in 1943. A new kind of musical, their model became the standard for a generation. More musical plays than musical comedies, they dealt with serious issues; characters changed and evolved via the songs, and every aspect of the shows worked together. Humor mostly came from characters and their relationships, rather than jokes. The music tended to draw from operetta, with sweeping romantic numbers and anthems. For nearly two decades, Rodgers and Hammerstein were the kings of Broadway, with shows including *Carousel* (1945), *South Pacific* (1949), *The King and I* (1951), and *The Sound of Music* (1959).

These musicals are just a stone's throw away from opera, so the vocalism here, often called "legit singing," is most like classical technique. But the addition of "theater" to the music means the words became incredibly important. While operetta favors open vowels and beautiful sound, and Jazz Age musicals favor consonants and clarity of the words, Golden Age Musicals favor both open vowels associated with the earlier Operetta genre, *and* clarity of words. As a result, a speech-like quality that matches the spoken voice became a hallmark of this style. But the raised soft palate and lower laryngeal position creates a warmer or darker resonance, and consistent vibrato is still expected.

The effects of this new standard for musicals can be seen in the works of Rodgers and Hammerstein's contemporaries: Irving Berlin with *Annie Get Your Gun* (1946); Cole Porter with *Kiss Me, Kate* (1948); Lerner and Loewe with *Brigadoon* (1947), *My Fair Lady* (1956), and *Camelot* (1960). Even as many shows of the 1950s pivoted back toward comedy, the songs stayed directly related to the individual characters and plots: think *Guys and Dolls* (1950), *The Pajama Game* (1954) *Damn Yankees* (1955), and *The Music Man* (1957). Vocally, however, these musicals were more affected by the doo-wop style, and incorporated more use of chest voice for treble voice singers and relied less on classical vocal technique.

Classic Musicals: 1960s–1970s

Starting in the late 50s, a new generation with their own unique aesthetics began to change the course of musicals. *West Side Story* (1957) was among the most controversial: it called for a cast of young actors-singers-dancers with violent choreography and difficult music. Leonard Bernstein created an amalgam of musical styles in *West Side Story*, drawing from operatic conventions. Kander and Ebb's *Cabaret* (1966) became known as a new type of show, referred to as the concept musical: shows that are less plot-oriented, focused more on ideas, milieus, and topics. *Bye Bye Birdie* (1960) introduced a mild version of rock and roll to Broadway. In 1967, *Hair: The American Tribal Love-Rock Musical* brought a fuller version of rock and roll, complete with sex, drugs, nudity, and controversy. Several of its songs became anthems of the anti-Vietnam War peace movement.

One of the most important figures in twentieth-century musical theater was Stephen Sondheim, who is credited for having reinvented the American musical with shows that tackled surprising themes, far beyond the genre's traditional subjects, with complex and sophisticated music and lyrics. Sondheim broke onto the scene (in collaboration with Kander) with *Company* (1970), a show that defined a new potential in musicals. Sondheim's reputation grew through the 70s (and beyond) and he became widely regarded as the greatest lyricist in the history of the musical, and among its most innovative composers. Still, the 1970s began a steady decline in the quantity, popularity, and success of new Broadway musicals, though there were certainly exceptions. *A Chorus Line* (1975), *Pippin* (1972), and *Godspell* (1970) all hail from this decade too and have stood the test of time. These musicals were based on a simpler book and presented simpler costumes and sets—they were not intended to be spectacles.

The biggest change in this era was not a musical or dramatic change, but a technological one. In the 1960s, body microphones became widely available. So much of classical singing technique is based on the need to project over an orchestra, and suddenly that didn't matter anymore. Any sound could be heard, so now any sound was possible. The genre started to shift rapidly to accommodate a broader range of sounds that could more creatively express a full range of human emotion.

Amplification made way for a wider adoption of the thrilling sound of belting, and audiences loved it. This style of belting, which we will continue to refer to as the "traditional belt," is exemplified by singers like Liza Minnelli and Barbra Streisand. Brighter and brassier resonance became more typical as vowels and diction became more conversational. Vibrato appears but is usually reserved for long sustained notes or phrases.

The introduction of rock brought with it a different kind of singing altogether. The vocal demands of rock, as utilized in shows like *Hair* (1967), *Grease* (1972), and *The Wiz* (1975), are similar to contemporary musicals of this era, but there is little concern for balanced registration or an even, consistent tone. In fact, the individual qualities of each register are used to enhance the style. Glottal onsets are utilized, consonants are sometimes highly energized, but often used colloquially, to the point that constants at the ends of words are completely omitted. Vibrato is rarely used.

Pop/Rock Operas: 1970s – Present

The late 1970s also brought the "British invasion," and with it the advent of the pop/rock opera. This style combines the grand nature of opera with contemporary pop/rock style orchestrations to create dense and emotionally charged works. Andrew Lloyd Webber is perhaps the best-known composer in this style, with hits like *Evita* (1979), *Cats* (1982), and *Phantom of the Opera* (1988), which is currently the longest running show in Broadway history. Other prominent examples are *Les Misérables* (1980), *Jekyll and Hyde* (1990) and *The Secret Garden* (1989).

Since many of the works in this genre originated with either British writing teams or did their original productions on the West End, there's a tradition of these pieces being sung with an even blend between pop stylings and classical techniques. While often sung by opera and classically trained performers, like Sarah Brightman, these songs are not meant to be sung in an operatic style. The tone is a balance between more forward resonance of pop/rock and the darker, vibrant resonance of Golden Age and opera. Vibrato, like in the Golden Age, is delayed, but is constantly spinning once it has started. But rock stylings are also common in this genre, particularly in shows like *Jesus Christ Superstar* (1970) and *Miss Saigon* (1989).

Commercial Influences:
Rock and Roll, Disney, and the Jukebox Musical

Movie musicals (Disney or otherwise) and jukebox musicals vary wildly from one show to the next, but they all have a common goal: to take some beloved music and/or story and bring it to the stage. Since these shows, like *Mamma Mia* (1999), *Movin' Out* (2002), and *Rock of Ages* (2005), feature music that already had lyrics, these productions add narrative while the singers work to match the sound of the original singer. That could mean emulating the smooth crooning of Frank Sinatra as in *Come Fly Away* (2009), or the iconic king of pop in *MJ the Musical* (2022).

Disney entered the theatrical arena in 1994, with the stage adaptation of *Beauty and the Beast*. Since then, Disney has become a defining presence on Broadway, with giant shows like *The Lion King* (1997), *Mary Poppins* (2004), and *Frozen* (2017). These adaptations typically add a new song or two—as in "Home" from *Beauty and the Beast*—but are generally designed for the audience to experience the same story and songs they already love in a new, live format. Singers, as with jukebox musicals, are generally striving to match the sound from the movie, so the ideal sound matches the era of the film. However, bright, forward placement is a common thread amongst most of these shows, as are character voices and the use of twang.

Contemporary Musicals 1990s – Present

The state of musicals in the modern era is an odd mix. There are of course revivals, jukebox musicals, and Disney shows, but some fascinating experimental works have also found success, such as *Light in the Piazza* (2005), *Spring Awakening* (2006) and *Next to Normal* (2009). There are also the occasional, country-sweeping megahits like *Wicked* (2003), *The Book of Mormon* (2011), or *Hamilton* (2015). And recent years have brought shows that bend and defy genre, like the jazz-influenced retelling of Greek mythology *Hadestown* (2019), or the reimagining of the oratorio form *Oratorio for Living Things* (2022). Pop and rock stylings have largely replaced the sound of the traditional show tune.

New terms have come into play to describe just how much things have changed, and how many options there are. In the contemporary legit style, singers use a brighter sound with less head voice, and chest voice dominance in the lower range. A contemporary mixed belt employs nasality and twang, and a contemporary heavy belt takes on a shouting quality. More and more, singers are expected to be incredibly versatile, capable in every style from operetta to rap. But there are some general trends, mostly stemming from the influence of pop music. For treble singers, head voice is used far less often, and the belt sound keeps going higher and higher. The high belt (above D_5) is no longer a rare novelty, but now an expected skill. Modal voices are shifting higher too, with high belt F and falsetto becoming more and more common in these roles. Vowels are nuanced in this style as they are frequently modified to meet the demands of pitch, range, and registration. But brighter vowels are the standard, rather than pure vowels, and straight tone is the default, rather than vibrato. Diphthongs and glottal onsets are the norm. Some exemplars of this style are *Once on this Island* (1990), *Songs for a New World* (1995), and *Kinky Boots* (2012).

Looking forward

> *You have two kinds of shows on Broadway–revivals and the same kind of musicals over and over again, all spectacles. You get your tickets for The Lion King a year in advance, and essentially a family comes as if to a picnic, and they pass on to their children the idea that that's what the theater is–a spectacular musical you see once a year, a stage version of a movie. It has nothing to do with theater at all. It has to do with seeing what is familiar. We live in a recycled culture… I don't think the theater will die per se, but it's never going to be what it was. You can't bring it back. It's gone. It's a tourist attraction.*
> – Stephen Sondheim[5]

Sondheim paints a somewhat bleak picture of the future of the musical theater genre, and in many ways the past 20 years have proven him right. Efforts to combat declining Broadway attendance—and boost profits—have resulted in shows that put a theatrical

[5] New York Times Magazine, March 12, 2000: pp. 40 & 88.

spin on stories and music that are already beloved: think the *Frozen* musical, or jukebox musicals like *Jersey Boys*. Revivals are big too, like the new version of *Oklahoma!* that reorchestrated the show to incorporate more of a country music style, or *The Music Man* starring Hugh Jackman. Certainly, many of these shows have offered something new to their audiences along with the old, but it is undeniable that the theater genre is not the consistent national influence of new ideas that it was in the last century.

We would argue that part of this continued shift is because of the internet and social media. Thanks to this democratization of media, very few things manage to capture the imagination of our entire country. Everyone can find exactly what they are looking for somewhere, so while something appeals to each of us, next to nothing appeals to all of us. Some shows start with ideas, stories, or music that already have broad appeal in the hopes of recapturing big swaths of the public. But others lean away, realizing that they too can rely on just a small group of folks that their show could truly speak to. Think about shows like *In the Heights* (2005) or *Fun Home* (2013); they didn't set out to appeal to everyone, but rather to truly speak to the experiences of a few, and to say something new.

We hope, and fully expect, that modern musicals will continue the tradition of providing social commentary that began all the way back in the 1700s with *The Beggar's Opera*. *Showboat* discussed interracial marriage at a time when it was still illegal; *Cradle Will Rock* powerfully examined labor unrest (so much so that it was almost shut down)[6]; *West Side Story* addressed gang violence and Puerto Rican immigration. Sometimes social commentary comes in a satirical package that makes it more digestible and perhaps more permeable, like in "Everyone's a little bit racist" from *Avenue Q*. But musicals don't always pull their punches, like in *Rent*, which puts the real-life cost of AIDS, drug use, and houselessness on full display. Musicals can be incredibly powerful vehicles for social commentary; shows with a bold message will be not only relevant, but also important. Performers who are prepared to speak to the social issues of our modern world with pathos and courage will be necessary.

---

[6] Reilly, Ann. "Musical Theater in America." The Kennedy Center, October 15, 2019. https://www.kennedy-center.org/education/resources-for-educators/classroom-resources/media-and-interactives/media/theater/musical-theater-in-america/.

Going forward into the rest of the 21st century, you can surely expect some recycling. There will be revivals of revivals, jukebox shows for today's popular artists like Adele or Bruno Mars, and probably an Avengers musical. But there will also be shows that are brand new, that speak to the truths of our modern lives, that no one can predict. So how do we prepare our students if we can't see what's coming? Unless you've got a crystal ball, the only solution is to train our students to be adaptable: arm them with knowledge of themselves and their instruments, the skills to fit themselves into new spaces, and the wisdom to maintain their own identities in the process. This type of teaching puts each student—and their unique personalities, competencies, and goals—at the center of everything we do.

Chapter 3: The Art of Teaching

Every book about voice pedagogy spends a lot of time talking about the function of the voice. Whether it is grounded in science or their personal experience, each author details their understanding of vocal function, and how all the moving pieces of singing fit together. We, as voice teachers, then take this information and tend to obsess about vocal exercises, and for good reason. The right exercise, when built from that understanding of vocal function, can deliver a singer to exactly where they need to be without words or lengthy explanation.

But as anyone who has ever taken a voice lesson knows, a great voice teacher is more than just a collection of vocal knowledge and effective exercises. They know both *what* to teach, and *how* to teach it. The ways in which a teacher imparts their expertise are enormously consequential to how the student receives it, or if they receive it at all: "If the students have not learned, the teacher has not taught."[7]

Many people assume that good teachers are born, not made—that these methods of instruction are primal instincts given to some and not others. We believe differently. Good teaching can be taught. Every teacher can become more knowledgeable not only about their subject area, but also how to share that knowledge more effectively. This book is dedicated to both the "what" and the "how" of voice teaching. Each following chapter will include a section about effective teaching strategies for a particular aspect of vocal technique. This chapter will explain our overall approach to teaching voice and invite you to examine *how* you teach someone to sing with a holistic approach. After all, it doesn't matter what is taught, but what is learned.

---

[7] Weimer, Maryellen. *Learner-centered teaching: Five key changes to practice*. John Wiley & Sons, 2002: 60-61.

Student-Centered Teaching

> *No matter how important the teacher may be to the development of a singing voice, no one has ever been taught to sing by anyone other than herself or himself. The singer cannot undertake the construction of a solid vocal technique without the assistance of a fine teacher, but in the long run it is only the singer who puts it all together or who fails to do so.* – Richard Miller[8]

Student-centered teaching is, put most simply, a style of teaching that focuses on learning, wherein what the student is doing and learning is the central concern. At first blush, it may seem as though one-on-one vocal instruction is inherently student-centered. After all, there's just one student in the room; who else could be at the center of things? Turns out, it's often the teacher. Most private music lessons operate through the master-apprentice model, wherein the teacher is considered the master from whom all knowledge flows, and the student the apprentice, whose job is to absorb the master's teachings. This model makes instruction one-sided, and it leaves students dependent on teachers for everything from vocal exercises to repertoire selection, to problem-solving in the practice room. It erodes their motivation to practice, as they strive to please the teacher instead of make music. It robs students of their creativity, as their unique voice and sense of expression gets sidelined in favor of the teacher's ideas and preferences. And, for students looking to find careers as singers, this style of instruction leaves them fundamentally ill-equipped for a field that requires incredible drive, resilience, self-reliance, and self-esteem. Many of us fall into this pattern because it's the way we were taught; after all, our teachers taught this way because it's the way they were taught.

We choose student-centered strategies instead for two main reasons: agency and equity. Student agency—the feeling that you have control over your own learning—is linked to higher achievement, as students who experience this feeling tend to take a more active role in their studies.[9] The equity inherent in this approach comes from the increased focus on students' talents and needs, as opposed to teacher expectations. Teaching this way prompts us to take an individual look at each student and treat them

---

[8] Richard Miller. *On the Art of Singing*. Oxford University Press, 1996: 28.

[9] Zeiser, Kristina, Carrie Scholz, and Victoria Cirks. "Maximizing Student Agency: Implementing and Measuring Student-Centered Learning Practices." American Institutes for Research (2018).

with respect. The shift toward student-centered teaching strategies in our voice studios is, in our view, necessary to responsibly educate young singers. But, because the master-apprentice model is deeply ingrained in our history and traditions as singers and music educators, it can be difficult to imagine another way. Here are five fundamental ways student-centered teaching can change your practices in the voice studio.

The Role of the Teacher

Practitioners of student-centered teaching often describe a shift in the role of the teacher from performer (sometimes described as "the sage on the stage"), to facilitator (or "the guide on the side"). Making the shift from performer to facilitator can be tricky for voice teachers, as many of us are trained and identify as performers! A simple way to start is by noticing how much you talk during a lesson, compared with your student. The goal in a student-centered environment is a relatively even balance, if not one that favors the student. If you discover an imbalance, ask questions. Rather than saying, "Keep the sound more forward," you might ask, "Where do you feel that sound resonating?" It's a less-direct approach in the moment, but the extra time spent up front will pay dividends later, as your student learns how to identify the issue on their own. Lessons can be laboratories instead of lectures; invite your student to experiment, explore, and ask their own questions.

The Balance of Power

What decisions are students allowed to make in your studio? Can they choose warm-up exercises? How about the focus of the lesson? What about the goals of your work together? In much of our experience, the student might choose what song(s) they sing in each lesson, but beyond that every choice is left up to the teacher. If a student is supposed to take responsibility for what they are learning, they must also have power over that learning. You can start with simple either-or choices, like "Would you like to try that phrase one more time, or move on?" You can invite them to make choices based on their own evaluation of their progress, mirroring the skills you want them to use in the practice room: "Would you like to do that one more time on a lip trill, or do you feel ready for the words?" As they get more comfortable with making choices and evaluating themselves, you can leave bigger decisions up to them, like constructing their own warm-up, or deciding if repertoire is ready for performance.

Students will make the "wrong" choice sometimes. There are moments where it's appropriate for you to step in and course-correct, like if the student is risking their vocal health (more on that in Chapter 11), or if consequences could be steep, like failing a class. But, more often than not, student-centered teachers let students experience the consequences of the decisions they make about learning. We all know that failure can be the best teacher.

Motivation

As voice teachers, when we think about motivation, practicing comes to mind. Many singers have a complicated relationship with practicing: in the long term, it's the source of growth, progress, and fulfillment; in the short term, it can be a source of boredom and frustration. It's no wonder some students struggle to find the motivation to practice. The good news is, many of the practices we've already detailed serve to bolster intrinsic motivation, like experimentation and student choice. We also recommend avoiding extrinsic motivators like giving rewards for practicing, or even tying practicing to grades. Instead, focus on what makes practicing inherently meaningful: growth.

Growth begins with efficient practicing, which looks different for everyone but may not be instinctual. Enlist your student in the effort to discover their best practicing strategies. Do they prefer morning, afternoon, or evening practicing? Do they prefer to have a set routine to follow, or do they thrive on variability? When do they get most frustrated? At what point do they find themselves getting bored or checking out? Only when they can explore these questions nonjudgmentally and answer them honestly can you devise an efficient practice protocol together.

We also recommend taking time to review your student's practice with them. Ask what they discovered that week, or what they found frustrating. This discussion shows them that their time spent in the practice room was worthwhile. Then, when you hear progress, call it out. Simply saying, "Have you been practicing that? It's much improved!" is enough to reinforce the habit—and it often leaves a student beaming with pride.

Evaluation and Assessment

Opportunities for evaluation and assessment in individual voice lessons vary widely depending on the setting. Maybe your students participate in an end-of-the-year recital, or maybe they're singing a role in a show. Maybe your students face juries or graded performance evaluations at the end of each semester, or maybe there's no formal opportunity for them to receive feedback. Whenever they present themselves, opportunities for assessment are important because they allow a student to see their own growth and the way forward. At least in your studio, these moments shouldn't be about grades, or the success of a show, or the opinions of others: these moments should center around the student.

Our advice here is simple: ask the student what they thought first, before examining feedback from yourself or others. This strategy serves dual purposes: the first is to strengthen their ability to self-assess. Secondly, allowing your student to be the first authority on their own performance keeps them in control of their learning and growth. When outside opinions and metrics define success, it's easy to feel like your progress isn't up to you—especially if those outside factors are fickle or subjective, as is so often the case for singers. Putting your student's opinion first gives them an anchor against the shifting tides of others' perceptions.

Teaching Technique through Repertoire

A key strategy of student-centered teaching is using content to teach skills; in the voice studio, that means using repertoire to teach technique. This approach can work particularly well for musical theater singers, who often begin singing lessons because they are excited and inspired by the repertoire and might therefore find pure technical work to be disconnected and joyless. This structure also allows you to explore technical principles through the varying styles of musical theater, so that your students' technique is appropriately flexible. But teaching through repertoire necessitates both choosing the right repertoire and working through it strategically.

Choosing the repertoire

Choosing the right repertoire is about balancing the level of difficulty. The best repertoire is difficult enough to encourage growth, but not so hard as to discourage the student. This necessitates getting to know the student and their voice, what they already know, and where they want to go, so you can identify the technical skills they'll need to build along the way.[10] The next step is to evaluate the repertoire. We look at the following aspects of each piece in determining its challenges, opportunities, and overall difficulty:

- ➢ Melodic Contour
- ➢ Registration and Style
- ➢ Phrasing
- ➢ Rhythm/Text
- ➢ Dynamics
- ➢ Accompaniment
- ➢ Harmonic language

Each of these aspects of a song can present challenges or opportunities. For example, does the melody have large leaps? Is there high belting required, or long phrases? Does the singer have to articulate quickly, or sing very quietly? Explore each of these aspects as you're working to determine how difficult a song could be for your student.

The final criterion for repertoire choice, and arguably the most important, is your student's preference. Students often practice more when they've chosen the piece, and we all know we sing better when we love the song.[11] So we suggest making your student a part of the repertoire selection process. We'll often chat with our students about their aesthetic preferences—what shows and songs they love, or which singers they idolize—and then pick a few songs that match those preferences and offer them technical opportunities. Then, we leave the final choice to them, with the option to send

---

[10] You'll notice that we didn't include voice type in our list of things to learn about your student. Too often, we assign voice types as a shortcut to understanding a student's voice, assuming that we can glean everything we need to know from the label "soprano" or "baritone." But even within voice types, every voice is different and warrants an individual appraisal. Voice types can be useful insofar as they help a student identify their strengths. But especially in the musical theater world, as singers are expected to do more and more, anything that puts a singer in a box and limits their vocal possibilities should be avoided.

[11] Renwick, James M., and Gary E. McPherson. "Interest and choice: Student-selected repertoire and its effect on practising behaviour." British Journal of Music Education 19, no. 2 (2002): 173-188.

Mackworth-Young, L. (1990). Pupil-centered learning in piano lessons: An evaluated action-research programme focusing on the psychology of the individual. Psychology of Music, 18(1), 73-86.

Sauerland, W. (2018). Voice class: A learner-centered approach. Journal of Singing, 74(5), 527-532.

us back to the drawing board if nothing we picked really speaks to them. Or you can start with your student's choices and evaluate the difficulty of the repertoire together. This activity helps your student build the incredibly useful skill of choosing appropriate repertoire. Additionally, if you find that your students are more knowledgeable about the repertoire in this genre than you are, starting with their preferences allows you to leverage their knowledge as you build your own lexicon of musical theater songs. If your student is completely enamored with a song that's out of their reach, you might choose easier sections to work on while building the skills they'll need to conquer the whole thing. We often use the terms "target" song (the one that is too difficult) and "scaffolding" songs (the easier ones that build necessary skills for the more difficult piece) to bring singers into the process.

Working strategically

The right song does a lot of technical work for you, but not all of it; the way you guide your student through that repertoire determines its effectiveness. Here are some strategies for maximizing the effectiveness of your carefully chosen repertoire:

1. Identify technical opportunities with your student. Make sure your student knows what they're meant to learn from each song, so they can focus on that skill and apply it across all their repertoire. Point out sections that may challenge them and spend time on those sections specifically in lessons, rather than always starting at the beginning.
2. Work on one technical aspect at a time. This slower, more deliberate process allows your student to focus on the issue at hand. Try starting with just a lip trill if air flow is the problem or speaking the words in rhythm if articulation is tripping them up. This slower, more methodical learning process might seem cumbersome at first, but it allows the student to build transferable skills.
3. Help your student develop explicit problem-solving strategies. Learning to sing relies heavily on repetition and practice work for which we as teachers can't always be present. Your student needs to know what to do when they encounter a roadblock and you're not around. Allowing them to problem solve in the lesson, with your guidance, will show them how to do so in the practice room.

Motor Learning

Much of the student-centered teaching literature we've drawn on here is based on classroom teaching. Singing differs from those subject areas in a few fundamental ways, the most consequential of which is that singing is a motor activity. In a voice lesson, you're not just teaching a student how to think, you're also teaching them how to move. Learning how to move our bodies, or procedural learning, is a different process from conceptual learning because it relies on the development of implicit memory.

Our ability to complete a task without consciously remembering how to do so is our implicit memory.[12] Implicit memory develops differently from conscious memory. We gain implicit memory not by *understanding* how to do something, but by *sensing* how to do something. It's all about perceptual cues—what we feel, see, and hear. Of those perceptual cues, we find physical sensation to be the most helpful in developing a reliable and consistent vocal technique. Visual cues are occasionally useful, like looking in the mirror to observe your posture, but often inaccessible, particularly during performance. Auditory cues are what we are mostly likely to focus on as singers, but the cues can change based on the environment, and often prompt singers to worry about how they sound, rather than focus on the task at hand. Sensation is more reliable, objective, and accessible to the singer.

Be careful of prescribing sensations to your students. Each body and every voice is different, so a lifted soft palate or a bright tone may not feel the same to your student as they do to you. Furthermore, we often rely on imagery to describe these feelings: "Feel as if you're biting into an apple," or "imagine you're waterskiing." But these images are associated more with cognitive meaning than they are with physical sensation and can therefore work against the development of implicit memory. Instead, we suggest inviting your student to observe their own sensation, identify it (verbally or simply in their own mind), and then either correct it, or chase it.

Utilizing this awareness requires the student to be "in the moment," and be able to pay attention to their sensations without becoming distracted. Allow your students to

[12] Verdolini, Katherine. "Principles of skill acquisition applied to voice training." The vocal vision: Views on voice (1997): 65-80.

focus on one area or function at a time; providing too many instructions at once can keep a singer from focusing adequately on any of them. Emotional responses can get in the way too. Observe your student's body language and tone and watch for signs of frustration or discouragement. Pushing through those emotions is rarely productive; switching your focus and returning to the issue in a more positive headspace will serve both you and your student.

Building Implicit Memory

Cultivating perceptual awareness isn't the only component of building implicit memory. Many different strategies can positively impact the development of implicit memory, some of which are intuitive and already embedded in the traditional methods of voice teaching. The first is repetition. This principle applies both in the voice studio and the practice room. Give your students multiple opportunities to practice new skills in their lessons and help them develop consistent practice habits.

Speaking of habits, combining acquired skills with other tasks is most successful when the acquired skills are habitually used. Alignment provides a great example: if your student is constantly slumped in their daily life, it's less likely any corrections you make to their position will persist when they start to focus on other issues. We suggest encouraging your students to observe their habits of voice use outside of singing. How is their body positioned while they sit at a desk, or stand in a line? How do they breathe while speaking to a friend, or while singing in the car? All these habits will influence their singing work.

Specific feedback is an important part of the skill acquisition process; students need to understand how what they're doing relates to the desired outcome. However, more feedback is not always better. Interjecting after every repetition of a phrase or exercise can serve as a distraction from the physical sensations that form the bedrock of implicit memory. Allowing your student several uninterrupted attempts before offering feedback or instruction gives them an opportunity to better process and integrate new information.

Finally, implicit memory is context specific, meaning that it functions best in the environment in which it was acquired. Practicing in performance spaces is ideal; practicing in a performance mindset is essential. Whatever steps you and your student can take to replicate the performance setting during practice will help them do their best work when it counts. Still, you can't perfectly prepare for every eventuality of live performance, and our larger goal is that students can easily and consistently apply their skills to new repertoire and in new environments. Generalizable skills require variable practice. We recommend attacking a new technique from multiple angles: use exercises that incorporate various vowels, tempi, phrases, and styles.

Encouraging Creativity

Imagination is an essential prerequisite of singing—not an optional extra.
– Thomas Hemsley[13]

In classical singing—the tradition from which many of our ideas about teaching voice come—there is a standard sound that a student needs to learn to make. But in musical theater, singers are expected to make a huge variety of sounds in service to the text and the character. Thomas Hemsley's above quote about imagination becomes relevant here because the choices we make about how we sing in musical theater must be inextricably linked to the story we're telling. Creativity is at the heart of the genre, and it should live at the heart of the way we teach it.

The trouble is that the traditional ways we teach voice (through the master-apprentice model, after historic methods of classical singing training). In the classic tradition) often do more to quash creativity than to bolster it. When students get accustomed to simply being told what to do at every turn, it becomes harder to make their own choices. When the teacher is always right, students learn to quiet their own artistic instincts. When everything they do is either right or wrong, the singer's ability to explore and discover is lost in a fervent attempt to avoid mistakes. When we teach this way, we often end up with technically proficient singers whose performances lack vitality or spontaneity. We say they're just not performers, or that they lack "it" or "the x-factor," when really their x-factor—their individual imagination—was never given the chance to blossom. The American educational system, broadly speaking, operates

---

[13] Thomas Hemsley. *Singing and Imagination*. Oxford University Press, 1998: 111.

this way too, so students come to us already trained to think and learn by suppressing their creativity. To be truly effective teachers of singing, we must help students revitalize and reconnect to their imagination.

Adopting more student-centered teaching practices already is a step in the right direction, but there are lots of other ways to help your students be more creative. One important strategy is to encourage emotional connection and engagement during technical work. Asking students only to act or connect to a character or emotion in repertoire disconnects that repertoire from their technical work. In technical work, an emotional impetus can be a gateway to improved vocal function, like Jo Estill's use of the phrase "joyful shout" to describe belting.[14] You could ask your student how they might cheer on a teammate, or call out to a good friend, and turn those phrases into exercises. You could take phrases from dramatic moments of their repertoire and use those words in an exercise to imbue it with emotion. Or, you might have your student choose a different emotion each time they sing a vocalise and invite them to observe how their vocal quality changes.

When it comes to repertoire and performance, the goal is to help your student discover their character. Start by asking questions:

- Who are you?
- What do you want, and how are you going to get it?
- Where are you, and what's around you?
- When is it, and what just happened?
- What are you doing?

From there, the student can decide on the journey their character takes through the song. Ask them where the character ends up emotionally, and what changes happen throughout the song to get them there.[15] The key with all these questions is to allow your student to explore and experiment, and then to accept their answers even if they differ from your own interpretation of the song.

---

[14] Benson, Elizabeth Ann. *The Estill Voice Model: theory & translation*. (2017).
[15] Kayes, Gillyanne. *Singing and the Actor*. Routledge, 2015.

You may find that your students take to these creativity-boosting activities like ducks to water. You may also encounter some students who are uncomfortable with the vulnerability these exercises ask of them. We would argue that encouraging creativity is even more important for those students who are resistant to it. However, forcing a student to do something that makes them uncomfortable is a quick way to quash any burgeoning imagination. These students need an on-ramp: small, limited opportunities to make creative choices that will build confidence and trust. Invite them to pick one character question they find most interesting and zero-in. Asking them to sing with sadness or elation on cue during warm-ups might be daunting, so invite them to use their real emotions and try practicing next time they feel genuinely happy, annoyed, or otherwise emotional. If these small attempts are consistently met with affirmation, curiosity, and care, these experiences will build toward greater creative freedom.

The least creatively engaging aspect of learning to sing is often learning to read music.[16] Many singers see lessons in music theory as inexplicably mandatory, the result of arbitrary rules about what it means to be a musician. But studying music theory isn't ultimately about satisfying rules or passing tests; it's about gaining a deeper understanding of the music and how we might express it. Bringing your students to that deeper understanding begins with changing the way we teach this subject. Reconsider how you introduce the topic: instead of starting with treble clefs and note names, why not start with the expressive markings that offer clues to the character's state of mind? Or you could introduce chord quality, and then invite your student to explore why a composer might choose those sonorities and what emotions they convey. True musical understanding is, like the vocal mechanism, more of a web than a line. Your student can enter that web at any point that sparks their curiosity.

[16] We advocate that singers study western music notation not because it is superior to any other form of notation or to the aural skills required to learn music by ear, but solely because it helps many students learn music quickly. Learning songs quickly is both a practical and technical concern; the feeling of guessing about the pitches or the rhythm impedes air flow and generates excess tension. Practicing without confidence in the melody means practicing without freedom, so it behooves a student to quickly gain confidence with new music.

Brown, Kirsten. "Tonality and Technique: How pitch content affects the way we sing" Paper presented at the Voice Foundation Annual Symposium, Philadelphia, PA, May 2019.

Once they're asking their own questions, that curiosity can be your guide through the rest of the web.

If you're working with students who already read music, or if other teachers are responsible for teaching music theory in your program or institution, you can still influence the way your students use their knowledge. As they're making creative choices about their performance, invite your students to explore the sheet music. What do the tempo and key tell them about their character's state of mind? How do the rhythmic and harmonic structures affect the meaning of the text? Remind them that there aren't right or wrong answers to those questions, but each one offers a new opportunity to make a choice.

Artistry is about active, bold choices. A skilled performance is one in which the singer chooses specifically how to speak, sound, and move so that everything the audience sees and hears communicates the same message. We work toward technical prowess so that we may have vast choices about how to express sound. We work toward creative freedom for our students so they have the vision to see those choices, and the courage to make them.

Chapter 4: Alignment

The Science of Alignment

What is "proper" alignment?

The voice is the only instrument that is housed within our human bodies, therefore, the way we hold those bodies influences the way we use our instruments. Ideally, a singer stands with their feet hips-distance apart, loose knees, pelvis parallel to the floor, chest lifted, shoulders down, spine and neck lengthened, and the head floating effortlessly atop this relaxed yet energized structure. Ideally, a singer is not also dancing, or crawling, or wearing a five-pound wig. The reality of musical theater singing is that the conditions are often less-than-ideal for a singer's alignment.

Still, the efficiency of the vocal instrument depends largely upon the alignment of the body and its functioning in a state of poise. When unnecessary constrictions create wear and tear on the body, singers may experience debilitating misalignment. In an aligned body, the muscular system supports the skeleton and makes movement more efficient. The athletic nature of Musical theater singing requires a dynamic balance of muscle and bone and a volitional use of a support system involving muscles of the legs and torso that can handle the load of belting (more on that in Chapter 8).

So, what is a teacher to do? Some prescribe an ideal posture, knowing it will have to be compromised. Others prefer to troubleshoot and address their students' alignment only when it becomes an issue, and within the specific context in which it is causing problems. Different students may benefit from different approaches; some might need firm alignment rules to counteract bad habits, others may flourish with more bodily freedom to express and the occasional minor tweak to their stance. Regardless of how you choose to teach, it's helpful to understand the specific ways in which our bodies are connected to our voices, both to identify problematic postural habits, and to see when and how your student's alignment might be the proverbial wrench in the gears.

Connections to the larynx

The vocal folds are housed within the larynx, which is a collection of cartilages that sits on top of the trachea. Sitting directly on top of the trachea is the cricoid cartilage, often described as shaped like a signet ring with the face in the back. The pyramid-shaped arytenoid cartilages are perched on top of the face of the cricoid cartilage. The shield-like thyroid cartilage sits on top of the cricoid cartilage and forms the front of the larynx. The vocal folds run between the thyroid and arytenoid cartilages. The thyroid cartilage is connected (via the thyrohyoid membrane) to the hyoid bone—the only bone within the laryngeal system, and the only bone in the human body that is not connected to any other bones.

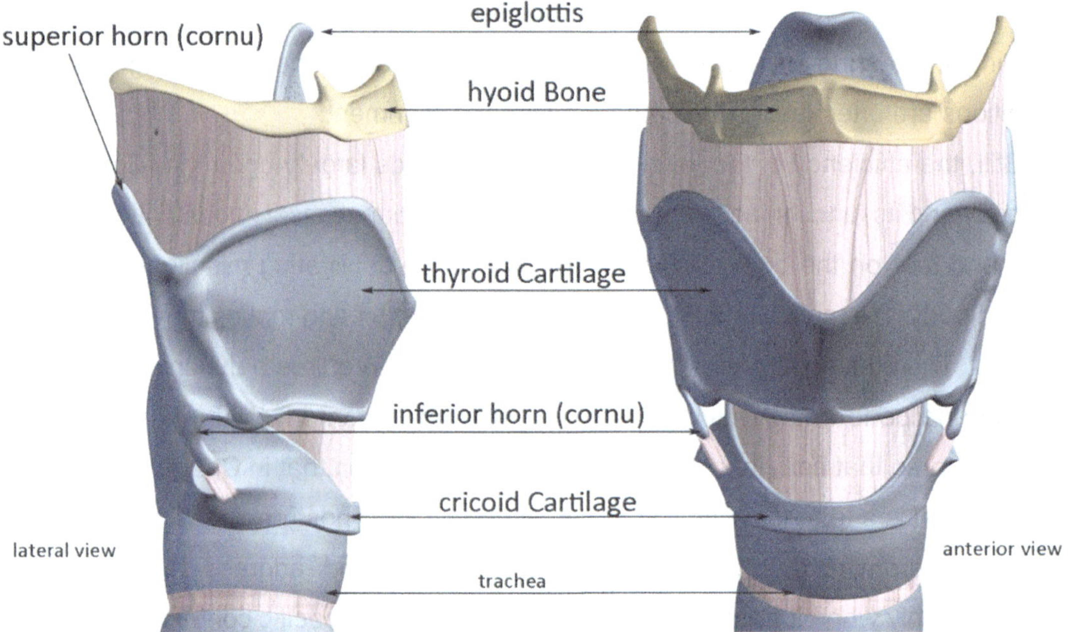

Figure 4.1 – Laryngeal system, anterior view

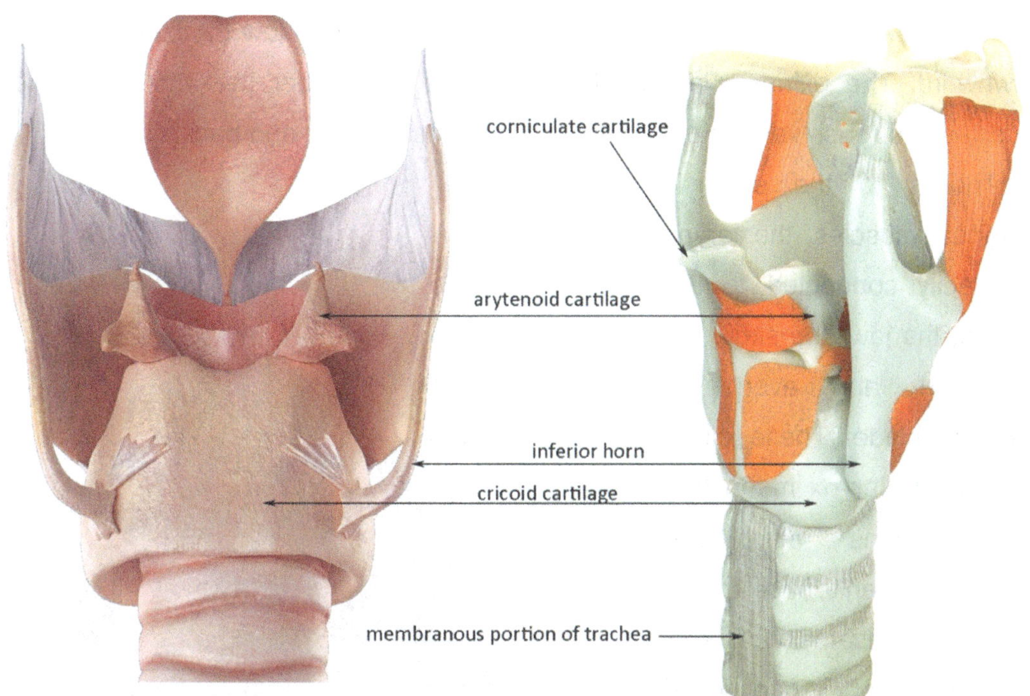

Figure 4.2 - Laryngeal system, posterior view

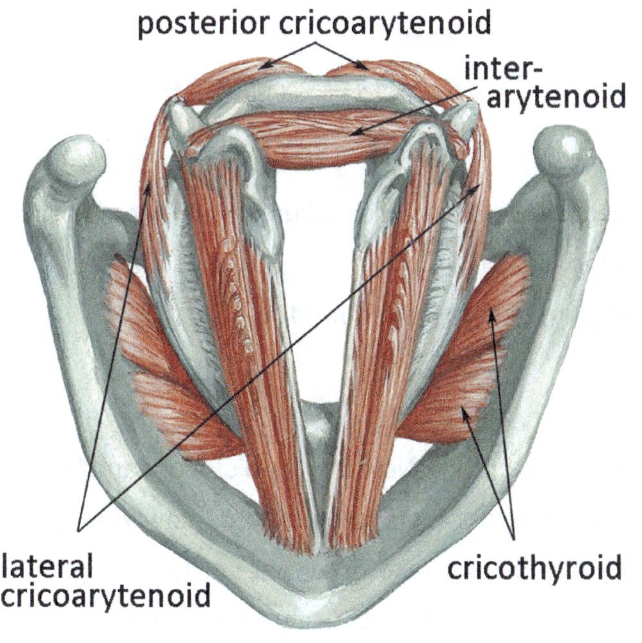

Figure 4.3 – Intrinsic laryngeal muscles

Netter medical illustration used with permission of Elsevier.

The fact that the hyoid bone "floats" is essential to the vocal system; it means the larynx can move up and down within the neck. To test this, put your fingers gently on your larynx and swallow—you should feel the larynx rise as your swallowing muscles contract and come back down as they relax. As we'll discuss more in Chapter 8, the position of the larynx within the neck is an important determinant of our sound. This position is the result of the muscles that connect to the larynx, broadly referred to as the extrinsic laryngeal muscles. These muscles fall into two categories: the suprahyoid muscles that attach above the larynx and lift it upward, and the infrahyoid muscles that attach below the larynx and pull it downward. The extrinsic laryngeal muscles far outnumber the intrinsic laryngeal muscles and reach various points on the face, neck, chest, and back.

Thanks to the extrinsic laryngeal muscles, the larynx is directly connected to the tongue, the jaw, the skull, the rib cage, and even the shoulder blade. These direct lines to the larynx mean that the positions of these structures aren't ancillary or aesthetic concerns, but real determinants of the quality and sustainability of our singing. Let's take head position as an example; many students have been cautioned against raising the chin too high, and consequently tuck their chin when singing. Both extremes influence laryngeal position: an overly tucked chin may keep the larynx too low and raising the chin may pull it too high. As with so many aspects of singing, balance is required.

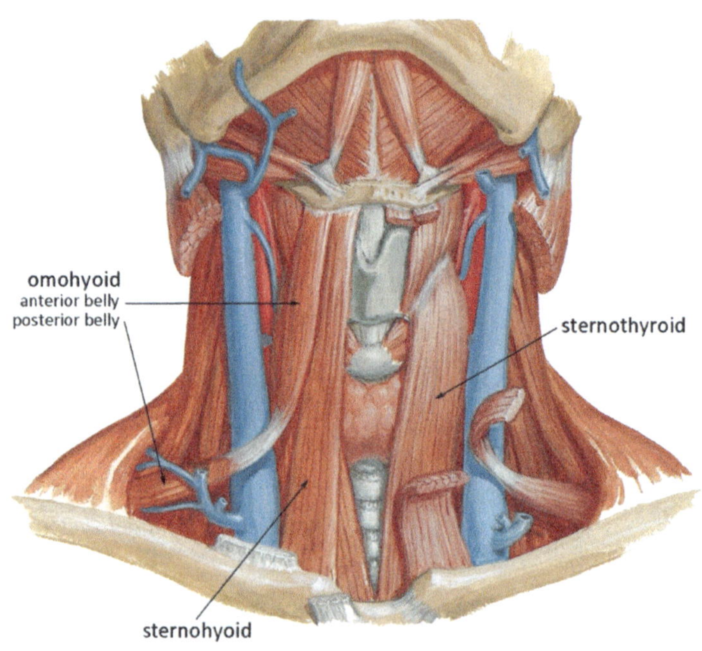

Figure 4.4 - Extrinsic laryngeal muscles

Connections to the respiratory system

Try this experiment: slouch and take a deep breath. Now stand up straight and breathe deeply again. Do you notice how much easier it feels to breathe deeply when you're standing up straight and how much more air you take in? What you're feeling is just how profoundly our respiratory system is connected to our body's position. For reasons we'll explore in the next chapter, the size and shape of our lungs is directly controlled by the position of our rib cage. The way we move our shoulders also contributes to the size of the chest cavity, and some of the muscles in our back can play a large role in support (more on that in Chapter 7). The abdomen matters too, and how available that space is plays a large role in how much air we can take in and how we manage that air on the way out.

Connections in the lower body

Have you noticed that most voice teachers describe ideal posture from the bottom up? That's because the position of our lower body determines how we can balance our weight. And since nearly every structure in our body (except our organs) can be recruited in our constant struggle against gravity, how we position our feet, legs, and pelvis can have ripple effects throughout our bodies. Try singing while standing on one foot. How about while leaning forward, back, or to one side? Notice how your abdominal muscles and upper body respond to these different positions and work to keep you upright. How does that affect your singing?

A few areas in the lower body are worth giving special attention regarding finding and keeping balance. We'll start at the bottom with the feet. Hips-distance apart is most often prescribed position because it allows the weight to flow down from the hips in a straight line. Too wide or too narrow of a stance means that muscles of the legs must work harder to maintain balance. Keeping knees and ankles loose also helps maintain optimal function of the leg muscles—locking the knees may also cause fainting, as it blocks blood vessels and allows blood to pool in the legs.

The position of the pelvis also strongly influences our balance. The hip joints are the midpoint of our bodies (from top to bottom). As a result, the position of the pelvis affects both how our weight is stacked above it, and how it is distributed below. Ideally, the pelvis is parallel to the floor, not tilted too far forward, back, or to one side. This neutral position allows our upper body to sit comfortably on top of our lower body. Without this neutral position, excess muscular activity is needed to keep us standing tall. Imagine a layer cake with a tilted middle layer, and what a baker might have to do to keep the upper layers on top of that cake.

Tension and flexibility

> *Muscles do two things—they tense, and they relax. In order for muscles, including singing system muscles, to do work, they must tense. The question then becomes, 'How much does a muscle need to tense in order to do the job it is asked to do?'* – Robert Edwin[17]

The danger inherent in each of these connections is excess tension. Singers and voice teachers alike frequently throw around the word "tension" as a vague, catchall term for anything bad or wrong about someone's singing. So, let's be specific: muscle tension is when a muscle remains semi-contracted for an extended period. Far from free movement and productive muscular engagement, tension indicates a muscle is locked in place, not allowed to fully contract or relax. Tension around the respiratory system means breath can't flow easily or freely. Tension around the larynx means the vocal folds can't vibrate easily or freely, which can lead to vocal injury (more on that in Chapter 11).

Tension sits opposite flexibility. Think of flexibility not just as the ability to touch your toes or do the splits, but as a broader measure of how free our bodies are to move. If tension is what we are avoiding as we carefully curate our body's position, flexibility is what we are striving for. Even the ideal position—feet hips-distance apart, loose knees, pelvis parallel to the floor, chest lifted, shoulders down, spine and neck lengthened, and balanced head—fails if the singer is locked in place. The condition of flexibility, of being energized and ready for movement, is more important than the strict position of any part of the body. In that sense, functional singing posture can be achieved even while dancing, crawling, or wearing a five-pound wig.

---

[17] Elizabeth Ann Benson. *Training Contemporary Commercial Singers*. Compton Publishing, 2020: 84.

The Art of Alignment

> *In order to express a most delicate and largely subconscious life, it is necessary to have control of an unusually responsive and excellently prepared vocal apparatus... That is why an actor of our type is obliged to work so much more than others, both on his inner equipment, which creates the life of the part, and also on his physical (vocal) apparatus, which should reproduce the results of the creative work of his emotions with precision* – Constantin Stanislavski[18]

The voice reflects both the physical condition of the body and the personality of the singer. In Musical theater characters, every type of physical life exists, and the physical body is part of the performance. Any posture is reasonable and potentially efficient if the muscles are free for movement, leaving the skeleton to "carry the load." That movement doesn't just support the technical aspects of a singer's performance, it is integral to the emotional aspects as well. Feelings present themselves in vocal sounds as well as physical movement: it is impossible to separate the two. Thus, a singer who seeks to improve their alignment is best served not just through physical correction, but also through attention to their intention and imagination. After all, the foundation of truthful expression lies in the images and emotions that stimulate the body and the voice.

We often use the word *poise* to describe the ideal default alignment, the neutral state from which a singer can depart to authentically inhabit a character's physical life. Poise of the body is the prepared state of the instrument that is flexible, connected, lengthened, and energized. But poise of the body does not come easily without poise of the mind: a similar neutral state of being focused on the task at hand, connected to the music and words, and responsive to your emotional and physical landscape.

Our goal is to help singers find their own efficient dynamic alignment and balance as they work within their unique bodies. In Musical theater we are striving for tension-free *movement.* These singers are almost constantly in motion on stage. Nothing is fixed. We teach the singers to avoid constriction at the vocal fold level so they can sing (and dance) in any position. Singing requires a good deal of energy; it is essential that tension does not block the energy needed for the task at hand. We appreciate the

---

[18] Constantin Stanislavski. *An Actor Prepares*. Routledge, 1989: 113.

following postural analogy, specifically because of the movement inherent in it. You'll notice the author doesn't provide a static prescription, but rather a dynamic description of how one might position themselves and then move from, and through, that position:

> *With head and chest held high, and with an upright body, he sits on the saddle of his bicycle. With legs somewhat spread, he presses evenly on the pedals. By means of gentle rotation of his hips he, as it were, frees his upper body from all constriction, so that from this position he is able to steer his bike. Smiling and yawning, he feels a deep breath below the diaphragm, which produces a feeling of physical well-being. In this position he can enjoy his ride, and is also ready to sing.*[19]

In this description, the physical position of the body gives way to an emotional sense of well-being and enjoyment. Your singers can experience this phenomenon as well; the right alignment can lead to a more enjoyable, convincing, and connected singing experience.

The Art of Teaching Alignment

How can I talk to my students about alignment?

Terminology

The first question to address as you approach teaching alignment is one of terminology. Historically, voice teachers have used the word *posture* to refer to issues of body position. More recently, however, many teachers have shifted their vocabulary to the term *alignment*, as we chose to do here. The change is not in definition, but rather in connotation. For many students, posture implies a fixed and rigid pose. Using this term may introduce excess tension as the student struggles to constantly maintain a perfect posture. Alignment has a more generous connotation and can help the student view the position of their body as a series of flexible and balanced connections. Speaking of balance, some voice teachers choose to use that word as shorthand for this whole area; others favor body position or positioning. As we've discussed, flexibility is paramount, and the words we use to describe their position and, of course,

---

[19] Hemsley, Thomas. *Singing and Imagination*. Oxford University Press, 1998: 38.

the demeanor with which we address it, affects the degree to which your students allow themselves to stay free and flexible.

Awareness

The second question, and arguably the most important, is one of awareness. Two things distinguish singing from playing a musical instrument. The first of these differences is the role of the body. Rather than just providing the means of interacting with an external object, for singers, the body is our instrument. We strive to train parts of the body we can't see, muscles over which we often have no conscious control, and mechanisms and processes that are deeply tied to our survival. The beginning singer's first challenge is to become aware of these parts of their anatomy and physiology that they have likely overlooked for most of their lives. Once they gain awareness of these functions, you can begin to shape them together; if they can feel it, they can fix it.

There are many different approaches to alignment, especially so for musical theater singing as it places varying demands on a singer's body. But inherent in every approach is the necessity of a singer's awareness of their body's position (proprioception) and sensations. Some singers may enter your studio with a developed connection to their bodies. They may be able to quickly and clearly describe the sensations in their breathing, or in their throat. They may be adept at monitoring their own alignment. In our experience, however, a developed bodily awareness is not common among beginning singers and may not always be present in experienced singers either. Questions like, "Do you feel a change in your breathing?" or "Did you notice any change in your position as you sang?" are most frequently met with "I don't know."

But even when answered with *Je ne sais pas*, these questions are essential. Rather than just telling your student that you saw their sternum collapse or their head tilt upwards, offering them the opportunity to notice and discover for themselves will help them become more aware and independent. When you ask these questions, give them plenty of time to think about their answer, and offer them the opportunity to try singing the phrase or exercise again before answering so that they can more fully observe. Mirrors or video recordings also allow the singer to observe for themselves what's happening in their bodies, and utilizing a student's sense of sight can help them develop their proprioception. This approach may seem less expedient in the moment, but it will yield efficiency in the future as the singer becomes more able to observe and correct on their own.

Meditation practices are another path to developing this awareness. Mindfulness practices, like meditation, seek precisely to develop awareness, both internal and external, of the present moment. Many meditation exercises ask students to pay attention to the specific movements and sensations of the breath. Others involve scanning the body and noticing its positions and sensations, while others focus on emotional and mental awareness. Beyond bodily awareness, regular meditation practice may help your singers improve their focus in the practice room and better cope with the negative emotions that can often accompany singing training, like frustration, anxiety, and disappointment.[20]

For many students, a lack of bodily awareness comes simply from a lack of any previous focus on or training in using their bodies. For some, however, it can be a response to something more serious. For people who struggle with a negative body image or an eating disorder, observing their bodies can cause distress. Many trauma survivors experience a disrupted connection with their bodies and may struggle to feel sensations in certain areas.[21] For these reasons, it's important to be cautious when addressing your singers' bodies. We advise being mindful of these guidelines:

1. Don't express judgment about your student's body or appearance. Even compliments communicate that their appearance is both noticed and valued and may cause them to feel self-conscious or judged later, should their body change. Comments about others' bodies or appearances work the same way.
2. Be respectful of your student's comfort zone. When doing alignment work, be aware of their body language cues. Always ask before touching a student, and only do so when consent is given without hesitation. Be ready to move on if your student seems uncomfortable, distressed, or preoccupied.
3. Advise mirror use with caution. Using a mirror to observe the body can quickly devolve into negative thoughts about one's appearance, particularly in the practice room. Beyond being unpleasant, self-judgment shifts a student's focus

---

[20] Blackhurst, Lindsey Elizabeth. "Exploring the Whole Singing Self with Technique, Contemplative Education, and Mindfulness." PhD diss., Teachers College, Columbia University, 2021.

[21] Van der Kolk, Bessel. The body keeps the score: Brain, mind, and body in the healing of trauma. Viking Press, 2014.

away from their practice and all the sensations and movements you'd like them to notice. Keep mirror use targeted to a specific function and limited to a certain amount of time, and only advise this practice for students who have demonstrated comfort with it in your studio.

4. Don't try to be a therapist or probe too deeply into a student's discomfort. Simply provide a welcoming, non-judgmental environment, and allow them to share only if they wish. If a student shares some trauma with you, and they are not working with a mental health professional, gently encourage them to do so.
5. Never assume that any student has a positive relationship with their body. Body image issues, eating disorders, and trauma can affect people of any gender, size, or disposition.

Despite all the potential pitfalls, bodily awareness is an essential part of singing that must be addressed. Doing so with care for and attention to the student in front of you can help them develop not only their voice, but also freedom of movement, genuine expression, confidence, and a connection to and appreciation for their bodies.

What techniques and exercises are helpful?

There are lots of specific ways in which a student's alignment can be problematic, but in general, our enemy is tension. Tension is static: a muscle held in a state of semi-contraction. So, the antidote is movement. Movement can be applied broadly, like having your student simply walk around the room while singing, or it can be applied more specifically, like having a student who holds tension in their neck turn their head from side to side. The more freedom your student can find in their movement, the better. We've provided a few exercises below, but we also encourage you to allow your student to explore beyond our suggestions to find their own ways of moving.

Finding the Center of Gravity

A functional alignment is characterized by a sense of balance, or to put it another way, functional alignment relies on finding your center of balance. There are many ways to help your students find that feeling:

- Have them prepare to lift something very heavy, like a piano. In the moment before trying to lift it, they'll likely feel some muscular activity in their lower abdomen, in their center of gravity.
- Have them walk a few steps up a staircase, then turn, and walk a few steps down. Instruct them to notice the shifts in their balance that occur, particularly in their lower abdomen.
- Have them sit in a chair with their head in their hands and elbows on their knees and take a deep breath. This position should help them feel expansion in their lower back. Then have them stand up and try to find the same expansion in the upright position.[22]

Moving and Sound

Instruct students to move their arms and torsos, stretching freely and making sounds. Gentle sounds like sighs are best. They should stretch their arms over their heads, shaking their arms, legs, and entire bodies. Instruct them to "move with the sound," while continuing to phonate on a comfortable pitch.

Floor Exercise

The singer should lie on the floor with their eyes closed. Encourage them to feel the weight of their arms, legs, and buttocks on the floor. They should imagine that the space between their shoulders is opening and widening and that they are sinking into the floor. Climbing up the spine, one vertebra at a time, they will visualize space and air between the vertebrae. The spine lengthens and the breath keeps coming. Climbing into the middle and upper back and finally into the neck, which should lift out of the shoulders, the spine constantly elongates. The students should slowly rise to their feet, maintaining this elongated position.

Ragdoll

The singer should begin by lifting and stretching their hands over their head while slowly taking a deep, low breath. Next, the arms should swing gently forward and downward. This will lead the head and upper body into a bent-over position. The arms

---

[22] Hemsley, Thomas. *Singing and Imagination*. Oxford University Press, 1998.

and head will dangle loosely with the knees bent. While falling forward, the student should let air escape quickly on a high-to-low pitch, as in a sigh. Ask the students to hum and notice vibrations in their heads, maintaining relaxed sound with low deep breaths. They should slowly start to straighten up, beginning with the knees (not locking them), then the buttocks, slowly up the spine to the shoulders. The neck and the head come up last. The arms are lifted into a fully stretched position; the ribs should be fully expanded. Finally, bring the arms back to the sides, maintaining this expanded position.

Releasing Tension

1. As though lifting a heavy weight, stretch arms and hands out in front; tighten and release. Spread arms out to both sides; tighten and release. Pull shoulders up to the ears; tighten and release. Make a distorted, tense facial expression and release.
2. Rotate the shoulders forward, then backward two full turns in each direction. Notice the expanded rib cage when the shoulders rotate backward.
3. Stretch the head slowly to the left and to the right, looking over each shoulder, holding the position for five counts. Then while looking straight ahead, tip the head toward the left shoulder, right shoulder, and then forward, holding 5 counts per position. Let the jaw drop open when leaning the head left and right.
4. Begin with a "dummy-jaw" look and a blank facial expression. Yawn with the jaw stretched comfortably. Chew slowly and in an exaggerated manner. Move the jaw from side to side allowing the tongue to follow.
5. Stick the tongue out, roll it around, then side to side, and then up and down, as if you're licking ice cream off your face. Say yah, yah, yah and la, la la, etc.

What pitfalls should I watch out for?

When evaluating a student's alignment, the first thing to look for is ease of movement. Does the student look comfortable, flexible, and free? Or do they look stuck, locked, or tight? Beyond that general concern, there are a few specific problem areas to watch out for that affect alignment poorly and that can have ripple effects into other areas of the student's technique:

- ➢ Chin too high or too low
- ➢ Raised shoulders or one higher than the other
- ➢ Slumping posture with collapsed chest
- ➢ Too much curvature in the small of back
- ➢ Knees locked
- ➢ Feet too far apart or too close together

The first step in dealing with any of these issues is to draw your student's attention to it. Only after they feel it can they fix it. But it is in this corrective stage that the biggest potential pitfall of teaching alignment can occur. Drawing attention to a specific alignment issue can often lead a student to correct it with such fervor that they add more tension than they had in the first place. A student who's been told they hold their chin too high may then lock their head in place, or a student who's been corrected for slumping may hold their shoulders back as if they're a guard at Buckingham Palace. When dealing with these specific issues, you must go beyond just offering the correction. Help your student find a new position that is comfortable, that they can move through rather than be stuck in. Remind them that the goal is not to be statically, perfectly positioned, but rather to find a default position that is flexible, free, and conducive to their best sound.

Chapter 5: Breathing

The Science of Breathing

How does air get into the body?

For the purposes of this book, when we talk about "breathing" we're talking exclusively about the process of inhalation. As you'll see in Chapter 7, exhaling for singing is a complex process that merits its own discussion. For simplicity's sake, we'll start with the process of bringing air into the body before we delve into how we use it.

The process of inhalation begins with your primary muscles of inspiration: the diaphragm and the external intercostals. The diaphragm bisects your body and separates your chest cavity from your abdominal cavity. It attaches to the sternum in the front of your body, the 11th and 12th ribs on the sides, and the lumbar vertebrae in the back. It's a solid, musculotendinous sheet, aside from three openings in the middle that allow your aorta, vena cava, esophagus, and vagus nerve to pass through. The diaphragm has two domes, one on each side of the body that, when at rest, sit up inside the rib cage against the lungs and heart. Beneath these domes lie the liver, stomach, and spleen (or what we singers simply call the abdominal viscera). When the diaphragm contracts, the domes descend and flatten.

Assisting the diaphragm in the process of inhalation are the external intercostal muscles. They're called intercostal muscles because they run between the ribs, and external because they lie closer to the outside of the body than other muscles of the rib cage. There is a separate muscle in between each pair of ribs that originate in the upper rib and inserts into the lower rib.[23] When these muscles contract, they pull the rib cage up and out.

[23] A muscle's fibers run from the point of origin to the point of insertion, meaning that contraction generally pulls the point of insertion toward the point of origin. A gesture might be helpful in remembering this principle: imagine your arm as a single muscle, with the shoulder as the point of origin and your hand as the point of insertion. When you contract the muscle (bend your arm), your hand moves back toward your shoulder.

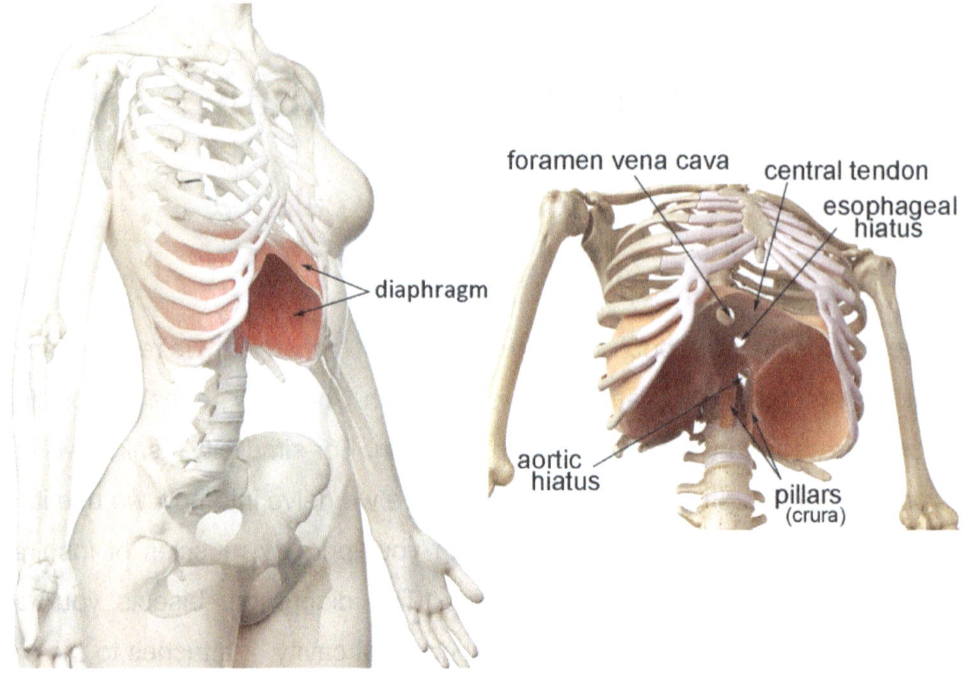

Figure 5.1 - Diaphragm, anterior and inferior view

The actions of both the diaphragm and the external intercostal muscles serve to expand the thoracic cavity, and thereby expand the lungs. The lungs are organs, not muscles, which means they can't expand on their own. However, the lungs are surrounded by the pleural sac, a serous membrane that sticks to the walls of the thoracic cavity like a wet plastic bag sticks to a window. So, when the diaphragm and external intercostals contract to expand the chest cavity, the lungs expand with it.

It is this expansion of the thoracic cavity that invites air flow, as explained by Boyle's law. Boyle's law states that pressure and volume are inversely related, meaning that a larger space results in lower air pressure, and vice versa. When the diaphragm and external intercostal muscles contract and thereby enlarge the chest cavity, the air pressure inside the body lowers. When the air pressure inside the body falls below that of the external environment, air rushes in through an open vocal tract to rectify the difference. This process is how you breathe every day, how you've breathed since the day you were born, and how you're breathing right now. Here's the short version:

1. The diaphragm presses down and external intercostals pull the rib cage up and out, expanding the chest cavity

2. That increase in space lowers the air pressure inside the body
3. Air from outside the body rushes in to correct the pressure imbalance

The difference for singing is the volume of air we take in, how we create the space in our bodies for that air, and habits that make the process of inhalation most conducive to the other elements of singing technique.

Volume and Space

Getting enough air is often a concern for beginning students; lots of young singers are afraid of running out of air, and as a result they strain to take in as much air as possible. Alleviating this fear is a great first step in reducing excess tension in your singer's performance, both physically and emotionally. Thankfully, most voice scientists and prominent singing teachers agree that the amount of air you take in is far less consequential than how you manage that air (which we'll discuss in Chapter 7 on the concept of support). An immense lung capacity isn't particularly conducive to great singing, and neither is a small lung capacity detrimental. The amount of air a singer needs is dependent upon the phrase at hand and the style in which they are performing. Too much air can result in too much breath pressure.

For the air we do need, we create space in our bodies for air to rush in, as opposed to constricting actions like "sucking in breath" or "pulling in air" to which beginning singers might be prone. Many singing teachers call this expansion-based strategy a "recoil breath," named for the buoyant sensation of suddenly releasing the abdominal muscles and feeling air rush into that open space.[24] Where and how we create space during inhalation is important and can have a big influence on a singer's technique. The three main areas in which singers experience expansion during inhalation are the abdomen, rib cage, and back. Many beginning singers may also make space by lifting their shoulders. While this kind of breath, often called clavicular breathing, can result in a greater air intake, it also can increase tension in the shoulders and neck and doesn't prepare the singer to support the upcoming phrase. Generally, lifting the shoulders during inhalation is discouraged.

---

[24] Kayes, Gillyanne. *Singing and the Actor*. Routledge, 2015.

Expansion of the abdomen during inhalation is the result of the diaphragm depressing and displacing the abdominal viscera that sit beneath it. Allowing the abdominal wall to relax and gently (not forcibly) expand during inhalation allows the diaphragm to descend more fully, which allows more air into the body. It can also have an effect on laryngeal position through the *tracheal pull*, in which downward movement of the diaphragm also pulls the rib cage and attached trachea and larynx slightly lower, which may not always be desirable in musical theater styles.

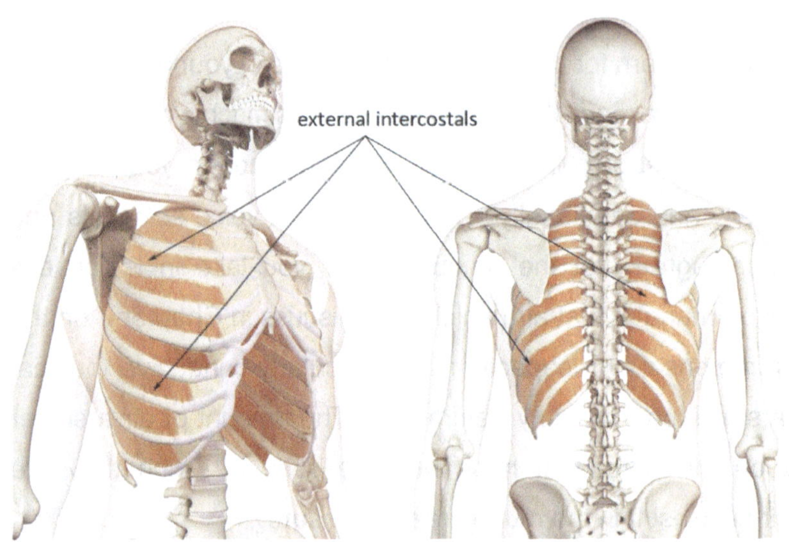

Figure 5.2 - External intercostal muscles

Expansion of the rib cage is the direct result of the external intercostal muscles pulling the rib cage up and out. Since the rib cage wraps all the way around the body, many singers strive to invite this expansion not only on the sides of their body, but also in the front and back. Just like with the abdomen, the more space a singer can create, the more air flows in. Expansion in the rib cage also prepares a singer well for supporting the upcoming phrase (more on that in Chapter 7). Breathing higher into the rib cage, almost feeling as if you're breathing into your armpits, may be helpful in establishing the appropriate laryngeal position and support for belting.

Some singers and singing teachers strive to promote expansion in the back. Expansion in the mid-back is the result of the movement of the rib cage and may also be aided by the latissimus dorsi muscles (generally responsible for extending and rotating the arms). Some singers also experience expansion in the lower back which, like abdominal expansion, is the result of the diaphragm's downward movement. Cultivating expansion of the back may offer a singer greater use of their powerful back muscles for support, as well as a fuller and lower breath.

Other effects of inhalation

The act of inhalation for singing can, and should, accomplish more than just taking in the necessary amount of air. The ideal inhalation is one that also prepares the body and vocal tract for the task at hand. As we will discuss more in Chapter 8, laryngeal position is a large determinant of timbre. Breathing in through a particular shape or configuration of the vocal tract (vertically, horizontally, and in the right vowel shape) can help singers begin each phrase with the correct laryngeal position for the style in which they are singing. Where classical singers might look for a comfortably low position of the larynx, musical theater singing generally requires a more balanced laryngeal position: not so low as to darken the timbre of the sound, but not so high as to restrict the tone. Strategies for identifying and maintaining this position will be discussed in Chapter 8, but keep in mind that finding this position during inhalation allows for a seamless start to the tone and helps prevent excess tension that may be introduced by trying to manipulate the larynx while phonating.

Another purpose of inhalation is to release any unnecessary tension that may be present in the vocal mechanism or elsewhere in the body. A relaxed inhalation can also influence laryngeal position and prepare other parts of the vocal tract, like the tongue or jaw, for the upcoming phrase. A free inhalation is generally a silent inhalation; any extraneous sound of air moving into the body is usually caused by excess tension restricting the vocal tract.

Many singers ask whether to breathe through their nose or mouth when preparing to sing. Although this decision generally isn't a make-or-break choice, breathing through the nose warms and moistens the incoming air, which helps the vocal folds stay hydrated. However, the nasal passages are narrower than the oral cavity, so air doesn't enter the body quite as quickly through the nose. For quick inhalations between phrases, trying to breathe solely through the nose might result in excess tension as the singer tries desperately to get enough air in a short amount of time. On these occasions, the singer should breathe through their mouth as well.

The Art of Breathing

> *If the singer can feel their bodies as vibrating instruments (like the body of a cello) which must be activated and set in vibration, then they have already gone a long way toward achieving balanced animation. The control of breathing can then come naturally, in response to the singer's 'impulse' or 'intention.'* – Thomas Hemsley[25]

Feeling and breathing are related parts of the communicative experience. Any singer who is psychologically inhibited, will find free respiration a problem, consequently inhibiting vocal freedom. Conversely, the singer whose breathing is free and coordinated, will have an invaluable tool to connect to their emotions through singing. As a result, it is imperative that efficient and coordinated respiratory skills be developed. The types of adjustments necessary depend in part on what the singer is thinking and feeling. The breath must be responsive to the thought one is trying to express, and to the emotion that goes with it.

One of the reasons that so many breathing techniques exist in voice training, is the fact that there are so many ways to breathe. The equipment is designed so that flexibility of its use is part of our natural adaptability to changing circumstances. We change our breathing in response to emotion, and each emotion has its own breathing pattern. The control of breath is performed by the whole body, and guided by the singer's intention, stimulated by imagination. It is the feeling that comes from maintaining the whole being in the state of readiness; a state of expectant stillness, together with the joyful feeling associated with the desire to say something tremendous.

To explore this idea, try breathing through different emotions. Breathe as if you are about to express joy, then anger, then sadness, then disgust, then fear. How does your body move differently in each distinct emotional state? Are certain emotions more conducive to a free breath? We've found that exhilaration is a particularly useful emotion for breath work, as it results in both an energized and open inhalation. But of course, this only works if the phrase that follows expresses a similar emotion. Part of breathing work, particularly in the musical theater genre, is finding methods of

---

[25] Hemsley, Thomas. *Singing and Imagination*. Oxford University Press, 1998: 41-42.

inhalation that work with specific emotions, so that the preceding breath is tied, both physically and emotionally, to the phrase that follows.

In finding these methods of inhalation, it is also important to consider the style of the piece at hand. Certain breathing methods work better in some styles than others, and it's important that your student's inhalation sets them up for success.

Traditional Legit

The traditional legit sound, being closest to a classical sound, benefits the most from a low breath. Because of the tracheal pull, a low breath can help a singer find a lower laryngeal position, resulting in the resonance and vocal colors associated with the classical style.

Contemporary Legit

Contemporary legit singing is often conversational, with short phrases located within speech range. For this style of singing, a focus on breathing may not be entirely necessary. If the student employs a healthy breathing pattern for speech, you may find that their natural breathing habits are entirely sufficient for this style. Overanalyzing the inhalation may not be helpful in these instances.

Traditional and Contemporary Belt

For reasons we'll discuss in more detail in Chapters 6 and 8, belting relies on a neutral, perhaps even slightly elevated laryngeal position. This means that a low breath that relies predominantly on abdominal expansion may be unhelpful. Consider locating most of the expansion in the rib cage and back for this style of singing. Think of the expansion as being under the armpits. The shoulders and clavicle should not rise.

The Art of Teaching Breathing

How can I talk to my student about breathing?

Everyone already knows how to breathe. Since the moment we were born, our bodies have handled this most basic function without much need for conscious intervention. It is for this reason that some voice teachers, especially in the musical theater genre, choose not to focus on breathing with their students, relying instead on their students' natural ability to breathe, combined with the emotional stimulus of the repertoire at hand. For some students, this approach works well. If their method of breathing is serving them, there is little to be gained in dismantling and over-explaining that function. If it ain't broke, don't fix it.

It's important to remember, however, that breathing simply to sustain life and breathing for singing are two different things. Breathing for singing requires a shorter inhalatory phase, a much longer exhalatory phase, and enough air pressure to sustain phonation at varying pitch levels. A perfectly efficient resting breath, or even an excellent breath pattern in speech, will not necessarily translate to singing.

So how do you know if your student's breathing needs attention? Ask your student to take a deep breath, as if for a long note, and watch what happens in their body. Do their shoulders rise? Do you hear a noisy inhalation? Do you see excess tension in their neck or jaw as they try desperately to suck in air? All these things are indicators of an inefficient inhalation that needs to be addressed.

A discussion of the science that makes this kind of breath possible can be helpful for many students. Understanding the basics of volume, space, and pressure within our respiratory system can help your students identify their impulse to suck in air as not just improper technique, but as superfluous and detrimental to their best breath.

Keep in mind that expanding the body in this way will likely be foreign to many students. Relaxing the abdominal muscles can be difficult, as many people unconsciously maintain constant contraction in the abdominal muscles. For some, this omnipresent tension is the result of training as a dancer or other kind of athlete. For others, this habit stems from family members' admonishments to "suck it in," or from societal messaging to appear thinner. Musical theater industry expectations don't help, as they often demand slim physiques and flat tummies. Learning to release abdominal tension during inhalation and allowing the abdomen to gently expand can be a vulnerable endeavor for some students and should be approached thoughtfully. If you have also found it difficult to expand your abdomen, share that with your students as you're comfortable—it may help them navigate their own feelings of vulnerability. Giving them explicit permission to take up more space may also be helpful, particularly for your students who identify as women.

Beyond these basics of breathing, the right breathing strategy is different for each style, song, and even phrase. As we've referenced, an inhalation that works well for a legit piece might cause problems for belting, or vice versa. To explore the impact of breathing on laryngeal position, try breathing in through an "uh" vowel with your fingers on your larynx. You'll likely notice a slight downward motion. Then try "ah" —you should feel the larynx remain stable. Finally, breathe through an "ae" sound (as in "cat") to feel the larynx rise slightly.

What techniques and exercises are useful?

One way to start is by helping your student experience a breath initiated by expansion, rather than a sucking or pulling sensation. This exercise, borrowed from Gillyanne Kayes, can introduce your student to that sensation:[26]

1. Put one hand over your abdomen. Your thumb should be roughly over your navel.
2. Breathe out sharply on the sound 'PShhh.' Use your hand to send the abdomen right back toward your backbone. Don't bother to breathe in for this exercise—you always have air in your lungs. Just concentrate on this energetic exhalation.
3. Notice that if you wait and allow your abdominal wall to relax at the end of the sound, the abdomen will bounce outwards, and you will have breathed in.

If your student is having trouble releasing their abdominal muscles, try a sigh of relief. Have the student imagine lying down at the end of a long day and breathe out as if they've just laid their head on their pillow. For many of us, this moment is one wherein we release our air in a long sigh, rather than pushing it out. The inhalation that follows is also likely to be released and free.

To facilitate this easy flow between inhalation and exhalation, have your student practice breathing in for four counts and then immediately, without stopping, exhale for four counts. See if they can eliminate any sense of a pause or stop between the

---

[26] Kayes, Gillyanne. *Singing and the Actor*. Routledge, 2015.

inhale and exhale; that can be a moment for excess tension to infiltrate the breathing process.

Once they've accomplished that exercise, add a vowel sound to the exhalation. We like the schwa. Then you can extend the schwa for eight counts. Finally, add an easy pitch in the middle register.

We share many more exercises on breathing, particularly those that relate to an efficient exhalation, in Chapter 7. All those exercises will function more effectively, however, if they begin with a relaxed, efficient, and expanded inhalation.

Breathing and the Flowchart

Breathing and Alignment

You can't separate breathing from alignment. It's one and the same. If the body is prepared and organized, the breath will flow. – Joan Lader[27]

Since appropriate breathing for singing relies on expansion in key areas of the body, the position of those areas of the body has a massive impact on how we inhale. To see for yourself, try taking a deep breath while seated, standing upright, standing slumped, and lying down. You'll likely notice differences in how much air you took in, as well as the sensation of the breath in your body.

Appropriate alignment for musical theater singing is, as we discussed in the previous chapter, not a static position, but rather a moving target that must be both technically viable as well as supportive of the character and mood of the song at hand. A large part of that technical viability is how any given position or movement affects the singer's ability to breathe and find the necessary expansion in their body. For more conversational singing, this may be less of a concern. For climactic moments, the interplay between breathing and alignment may suddenly become paramount to your

---

[27] Melton, Joan. Singing in musical theatre: The training of singers and actors. Simon and Schuster, 2010: 33.

student's success. Determining the style of breathing necessary for a song, or even phrase, may help your student determine what postures or movements are viable, or even necessary, to support their performance. Helping your student pay attention to the way they need to breathe can help them be more aware of how they need to align their body.

Chapter 6: Phonation

The Science of Phonation

What is phonation?

Science's best guess is that the vocal mechanism did not evolve for the purpose of producing speech. At their most fundamental level, the vocal folds function as a valve, sealing off the chest cavity so the necessary air pressure can build up for strenuous activities like lifting heavy objects, defecating, or childbirth. They also act as a last-ditch barrier to keep any food or drink from reaching the trachea and lungs. The fact that the vocal folds, when put under less pressure, can vibrate and produce sound seems like a happy evolutionary accident.

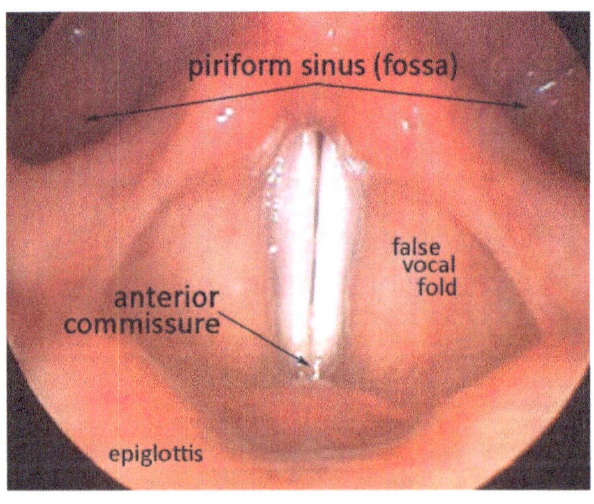

Figure 6.1- Vocal folds, superior view

In this book, the term phonation will refer to the opening, closing, and vibrating of the vocal folds. The vocal folds are positioned just over the trachea, stretching between the thyroid and arytenoid cartilages that help make up our larynx. When at rest, they are shaped like a V, with the point of that V at the front of the neck and the two ends toward the back. The space between the vocal folds is referred to as the glottis. The glottis is open during inhalation, to allow air into the trachea, and closed during phonation. The picture above is of closed vocal folds, as in during phonation, positioned from above, with the front of the neck at the bottom.

How does phonation start?

For phonation to occur, the vocal folds must first come together. Two sets of muscles work to bring the arytenoid cartilages together, which closes the V into a straight line. The lateral cricoarytenoids rotate the arytenoid cartilages, which helps to bring the middle of the vocal folds into contact. The interarytenoid muscles pull the arytenoid cartilages toward each other, closing the back of the glottis.

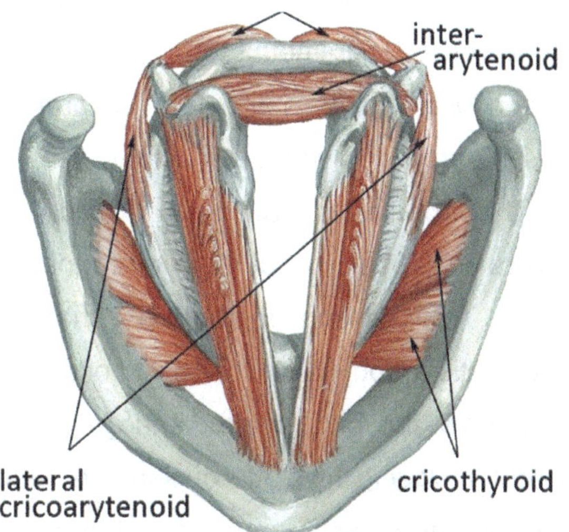

Figure 6.1 - Abductor and adductor muscles

Netter medical illustration used with permission of Elsevier.

Exhalation begins with the thoracic cavity shrinking and air pressure raising inside the thoracic cavity. Once enough pressure has built up, an amount referred to as phonation threshold pressure, the air blowing through our closed vocal folds sets them into motion. The vocal folds vibrate from bottom to top along the edge, and that vibration ripples out across the area of the vocal fold.

The beginning of phonation, or the onset, involves both the coordination of air flow and the closing of the glottis. These two events can arrange themselves in a few different ways. The glottis can close before the air starts moving, which results in a hard or glottal onset as the air bursts through shut vocal folds. Or, the vocal folds can close as air is already moving, resulting in a soft or breathy onset where an "h" sound precedes the tone. Finally, many singers strive for a "balanced" onset, that brings the vocal folds together right as the air moves through them, resulting in a clean, but not harsh, start to the tone. We'll talk about the stylistic and pedagogical applications of these options in the coming sections.

How does vibration continue?

The vocal fold itself has a complex structure, but it can be thought of in two parts: the body and the cover. The "body," located in the center of the vocal fold, is the thyroarytenoid muscle. This muscle is surrounded by multiple layers of epithelium and mucosa that are broadly referred to as the "cover." The vibration of the cover is independent of movement of the muscle, or body. The cover's ability to vibrate and move freely is paramount to a clear sound. The importance of the cover is just one reason for a singer to stay properly hydrated; the mucosal layers of the vocal fold cover must be properly hydrated to vibrate freely.

This vibration is really a very rapid opening and closing of the vocal folds. Two factors keep this cycle of vibration running: elasticity of muscle tissue and movement of air. This explanation for the continuation of phonation is referred to as the myoelastic-aerodynamic theory of vocal production. Sufficient air pressure continually blows open the folds, and the springy nature of the vocal fold tissue brings them back to center, closing the glottis once again. Aerodynamics also assist in closing the glottis; the lower air pressure created by the quick movement of air through an open glottis also helps draw the folds back together (this relationship of pressure and velocity is known as the Bernoulli effect). Both the elasticity of muscle tissue and the movement of air enable us to continually produce tone.

All vocalized sounds, including sighs, grunts, whispers, and moans, are products of this process. It is not only the manner of closure of the vocal folds, but also the duration of that closure, that determines the quality of voice that is produced. One opening and closing of the vocal folds is called a duty cycle; the more the folds are closed during that cycle, the louder and fuller the sound. The more the folds are open, the lighter and softer the sound. For speech sounds, the vocal folds are closed approximately 90% of the time, whereas for extremely soft singing or speaking, particularly in head voice, the vocal folds may never fully close as they are vibrating. The ideal open/closed ratio will vary based on both the pitch level and the desired timbre (more on this in Chapter 8).

When we're done singing or speaking and need to breathe in again, the glottis must open. This action is the responsibility of the posterior cricoarytenoid muscles which pull the vocal folds apart as the interarytenoid and lateral cricoarytenoids relax. This movement of the vocal folds and opening of the glottis allows the air to freely rush in once the diaphragm descends, and the cycle can begin all over again.

Obstacles to vibration

The regularity and ease with which we produce sound in our daily lives can make phonation seem like a foolproof process. But things can go wrong, especially when we're attempting to phonate with the precision that efficient singing requires. Some of these problems arise from the way in which the glottis closes. Incomplete glottal closure results in breathiness, as extra air leaks out through the partially open glottis. Sometimes this effect may be intentional, like when one whispers, or in pop styles where a breathy quality is desirable, or in the extreme upper ranges. Breathiness is also common in adolescent treble voices; a glottal chink (glottal gap), or an opening at the posterior part of the glottis, is common during puberty and often resolves itself in later adolescence. Outside of these conditions, however, breathiness, may be a sign of a larger issue. Perhaps the lateral cricoarytenoids (LCA) and interarytenoid muscles (IA) are underdeveloped or lack coordination. Vocal fold lesions, like nodules or polyps, can also keep the glottis from closing fully. We'll talk more about vocal health issues in Chapter 11 but suffice to say that if a student experiences consistent breathiness, especially in conjunction with other vocal symptoms, it may be worth seeking the opinion of a medical professional.

Whereas some problems arise from not enough glottal closure, others stem from too much closure. Medial compression is the force that adducts the vocal folds, exerted by the LCA and IA muscles primarily. Medial compression can also be influenced by extrinsic laryngeal muscles (like the pharyngeal constrictor muscles we'll discuss more in Chapter 10) squeezing the vocal tract from the outside. When the vocal folds are pushed together with too much force, it takes more force to initiate phonation and it makes it more difficult for the vocal folds to vibrate. Thicker, stiffer folds and higher pressure often leads to a strident, pressed tone, and can sometimes cause discomfort for the singer. These conditions can lead to vocal injury if sustained for a long period of time (see Chapter 11).

What is vibrato?

Vibrato is usually defined as a periodic fluctuation of pitch, volume, and timbre. What causes it is less concrete, but most assume that a healthy vibrato stems from the way our neurological system interacts with our laryngeal muscles. This interaction is involuntary, meaning that vibrato isn't something that a singer *does* or adds to their sound. Rather, it is something they allow to happen. If the vocal folds are relaxed enough and the air flow is consistent, vibrato will be available.

Of course, in musical theater, we don't always want vibrato in the sound. But the availability of vibrato is a good indicator of healthy vocal function. The rate of the vibrato can also tell us a lot about vocal function. Vibrato that is too slow, often called a wobble, generally denotes an issue with support (discussed in the next chapter). Vibrato that is too fast, or a tremolo, is usually an issue of excess tension. While there are technologies that can measure vibrato rate (a healthy vibrato rate is generally between 4.5 and 7.5 cycles per second), you can rely on your ear to tell you if a student's vibrato is too fast or slow.[28]

The Art of Phonation

The emotion or meaning behind the sound begins in the brain of course, but the vocal folds and their various movements—stretching and shortening, bulking and thinning, the manner of opening and closing—contribute a great deal to the communication of the emotional content. There are many types of phonation, all particular to human expression, and the musical theater genre demands use of all of them so characters can express a full range of emotions.

So, while it is important to teach balanced onsets and coordinated phonation, it is also necessary to use these coordinations as a "point of departure" or a frame of reference for breathy onsets, harsh onsets, screams, laughter, etc. The vocal onsets greatly influence the character of a song, and there's no one correct approach. The "right" way to choose a vocal onset is to find the one that most effectively expresses what you need to express, provided it doesn't hinder the singer technically.

There are stylistic conventions regarding onsets. Glottal onsets in contemporary musical theater and classic character roles allow for a more conversational feel. You'll hear this type of onset often in rock and pop style musicals as well. Breathy onsets offer a feeling of vulnerability and intimacy and can add to the vocal characterization.

---

[28] Miller, Richard. *The Structure of Singing.* Schirmer, 1996.

The Art of Teaching Phonation

How can I talk to my student about phonation?

You may have noticed that we tend to use the term "vocal folds" rather than the more common "vocal cords." We do this intentionally because "folds" seems to be a more accurate description of our anatomy than "cords." When people picture their vocal cords, many imagine multiple strings like a guitar, or something that looks vaguely like the inside of a piano. You might be surprised to find how little your students know about what the source of their sound actually looks like and how it functions—for most collegiate voice students, this information doesn't enter the curriculum until their junior or senior year. Most young singers are essentially flying blind; their voices might as well be powered by pixie dust.

Depending on your student's level and interest, they may not need to know the particulars of the intrinsic laryngeal muscles, ab- and adduction, or duty cycles. But we have yet to meet a singer who is uninterested in discovering the basics of what's making that sound in their throats. Help them understand what their vocal folds actually are and look like, how they come together, and how they vibrate. Being able to visualize their instrument working can be immensely helpful in dealing with coordination issues. Imagining those little vocal folds vibrating freely can help a singer release some excess tension. At the very least, every singer deserves the empowerment and agency that comes with understanding their instrument and how to use it.

More so in this area than any of the others we've discussed, success depends on developing incredibly fine motor control and balance. So, a student's ability to work on phonation relies heavily on their ability to feel what is happening in their body. It's important that the student shifts from judging sound aurally to interpreting kinesthetically; encourage them to leave the listening to you!

What techniques and exercises are useful?

A great place to start is with a shapeless "huh" sound. Think about the way you might give a casual response when you're bored on a phone call: "uh huh." This doesn't take any effort or induce any tension. Once your student has found this primitive, easy sound, start bridging out into more complex sounds. Try it more quickly, like a pant, then on an easy descending pattern. Finally add vowels or even words, all while keeping that same sense of easy, instinctive phonation.

Efficient phonation creates a sensation of singing or speaking on the breath while avoiding excessive breath pressure or vocal fold tension. Easy phonation that has direction assists in finding that feeling, therefore exercises with a sense of momentum are helpful. You can use a sigh, or even a hum that expresses something, like agreement or the enjoyment of a meal! The colloquial affirmative and negative—"mm-hm" and "mm-mm"—are helpful.

Staccato exercises require coordinated control of the respiratory and phonatory systems. The goal is to apply breath energy while resisting the temptation to push, blow, or force air. Some light staccato exercises on five-note scales and octave arpeggios will help achieve this result. On a descending arpeggio (do-sol-mi-do) sing "How are you?", "He is Here!", "Whee", "Whoo" or other short phrases. Do the same on a five-note, descending scale.

Where staccato requires quick and precise coordination, sostenuto, or legato, singing requires consistency and maintenance. Start with hums or other semi-occluded exercises on elongated, simple patterns (like do, re, mi, re, do) in a comfortable range. Listen for consistent vibration and smooth transitions from one note the next.

It is necessary and important to offer techniques and/or exercises for singing straight tone, which is often preferable in much of the Musical theater repertoire. Since vibrato is an indicator of efficient vocal function, we suggest starting with a vibrant tone and moving slowly toward straight tone, to help the singer discover the very least amount of constriction required to remove the vibrato. It is beneficial if the singer believes that there is release and a tiny amount of vibrato in the straight tone. Crescendo/decrescendo exercises are helpful here. Start a tone in the easy middle range softly, allowing the vibrato to be present ("ee," "ay," and "ah" are usually most effective vowels to employ). Then, increase the volume while reducing the amount of vibration. Next, start on a forte, fully vibrant tone, and decrescendo while reducing the vibration so that the straight tone is sung softly. Vary the volume and the amount of vibrancy. Additionally, you can use staccato exercises on a single easy pitch and then slowly elongate the pitch, maintaining the straight tone.

What pitfalls should I watch out for?

Hypofunctional phonation

As we alluded to earlier in the chapter, hypofunctional phonation occurs when the vocal folds don't close all the way. The primary evidence of this problem is an airy tone. Wasted air is wasted tone and must be avoided. The thought of "the beginning of a hum" will bring about better vocal fold closure. Forward vowels, like "ee" and "ay" can also be helpful here. More importantly, the student needs more energy. The body is not providing enough support to produce a vital sound. Calling exercises are helpful: "Hey you!", "Not Now!", "Oh no!"

Hyperfunctional Phonation

Hyperfunctional phonation is the opposite problem: demanding too much from the laryngeal mechanism. Excessive tension in the vocal folds produces a hard, edgy tone. A common symptom of this fault is hoarseness. Corrective procedures should include relaxation techniques. Attention to incorrect breathing and over-support is also important. The back vowels should be used to combat pressed phonation; "oh" and "ooh" are less tense than forward vowels and therefore are more conducive to releasing tension. Combining these vowels with the beginning of a yawn is helpful, as is chewing while humming and adding movement, specifically in the upper body and neck.

Onsets

When you're dealing with consistently hyper- or hypofunctional phonation, swinging the pendulum the other way can be helpful. For example, a light glottal onset brings the vocal folds together before phonation begins, which can assist the perennially breathy singer in maintaining vocal fold closure. The sound "uh oh" is a perfect instigator for that kind of onset. Similarly, to aid the pressed or strained singer, adding an "h" to the beginning of the sound, like "hoo", gets the air moving before the vocal folds adduct, which keeps them from coming together too forcefully.

Vibrato

Sometimes, singers attempt to manufacture vibrato through muscular action in the abdomen or in the jaw and/or tongue. This strategy is not advisable as it leads to excess tension and, generally, either a wobble or tremolo. If a student is having trouble producing vibrato naturally, start by working on support and alleviating excess tension. There are also some examples of vibrato in speech that may help a student find their vibrato, like a passionate preacher saying, "Oh Lord!", a dramatic speech from a politician, or imitating the sound of a spooky ghost.[29] If the student can mimic these moments in speech, the transition to singing is usually simple. Finally, quick exercises with repeating or oscillating pitches may help the vibrato emerge.

Phonation and the Flowchart

Phonation and Alignment

We mentioned above that medial compression (the force that pushes the vocal folds together) can be influenced by muscles outside of the larynx. Too much tension in the neck and pharyngeal constrictor muscles can push the vocal folds together from the outside, resulting in a harsh and pressed tone. Sometimes this tension is the result of poor alignment, and of muscles in the neck having to work harder than normal to keep the head sitting atop the spine. If you're hearing pressed phonation, observe your student's body: is how they're positioned creating excess tension in the upper body? If so, fixing their alignment might begin to alleviate the problem.

Phonation and Breathing

One of the conditions for an ideal breath, as we said in the previous chapter, is silence during inhalation. A silent breath indicates nothing is blocking the path of the air as it travels into the body, including the vocal folds. For a silent inhalation to occur, the

[29] Ibid.

vocal folds must abduct all the way, fully opening the glottis. Helping your students combine their inhalatory technique with an open throat is a great way to release excess tension, even tension that may have built up during the previous phrase and offer your student a laryngeal reset.

Chapter 7: Support

The Science of Support

What is support?

The word "support" is ubiquitous in voice studios, and yet it means something completely different to many voice teachers. In the most basic terms, support involves how we exhale for singing. Since exhalation is the power source of our instrument, how we support our voice influences every other area of vocal technique. But support is not a catch-all or a cure-all—only a teacher who understands precisely what they are asking their student to do can effectively employ the concept of support. A vague concept of support often serves to confuse and frustrate students, which is why some teachers avoid this terminology entirely and opt instead for phrases like "breath control" or "breath management." Whatever terminology you choose to refer to this process, it is helpful to understand the physiological realities of exhalation and how they shape our singing.

How do we exhale?

The way we exhale when at rest, likely the way you are exhaling right now, is essentially a reversal of the process of inhalation. The diaphragm and external intercostal muscles relax and return to their at-rest positions, which decreases the volume of the chest cavity. This decrease in volume leads to an increase in air pressure, and air exits the body through an open vocal tract to rectify the pressure difference between the chest cavity and the external environment. Simple, right?

But exhaling for singing is a different animal than at-rest exhalation. In at-rest breathing, inhalation and exhalation make up relatively equal portions of the breath cycle, meaning inhalation and exhalation take about the same amount of time. But when we speak and sing, the inhalation phase is generally shorter, and the exhalation phase is much longer. We take in more air more quickly, it must last us longer, and we need enough air pressure to keep the vocal folds in motion. Support is really about air pressure, and how we use our bodies to supply just the right amount.

What's the difference between breath pressure and breath flow?

Some of the confusion around the term "support" results from the conflation of the term "breath" with both breath pressure and breath flow. Breath pressure refers to the air pressure that builds up below the vocal folds, whereas breath flow refers to the air that passes through the folds. Imagine a water hose: when unimpeded, pressure is relatively low, and flow is high. But if you cover most of the opening with your thumb, the pressure increases as the amount of water that is allowed to flow through decreases. In this analogy, the thumb is your vocal folds. Thicker vocal folds allow more air pressure to build up beneath them, while thinner folds allow more air to flow through.

What is the right amount of breath pressure?

The right amount of breath pressure depends on the range and style at hand, but it hinges on the ability of the vocal folds to vibrate cleanly and easily. Too little air pressure and the vocal folds won't be able to vibrate. A singer might cope with a deficit of air pressure by thinning out the vocal folds so they are easier to set in motion, resulting in a softer, less full sound (more on this in Chapter 8), or by not fully closing the glottis which will result in a breathy sound. Too much air pressure risks blowing the glottis open and having too much air escape. More often in this scenario, singers thicken their vocal folds and/or more forcibly close the glottis using extrinsic laryngeal muscles, so that the folds can stand up against the amount of air moving through them. This configuration results in a pressed sound. Inconsistent air pressure that varies between degrees of too much and too little often results in excess tension as the singer uses muscles in their throat to try to compensate. The right amount of air pressure is the amount that makes consistent glottal closure and vibration possible within the bounds of the musical style at hand.

How do we find and maintain that Goldilocks level of air pressure?

Remember Boyle's law: volume and air pressure are always inversely related. By controlling the amount of space inside of our bodies, we can control the air pressure. Our primary muscles of expiration contract to decrease the space in our thoracic cavity, beyond what is accomplished by the relaxation of the diaphragm and external intercostal muscles. These muscles include the rectus abdominis, transverse abdominis, oblique abdominis, internal intercostals, and some muscles of the back as well.

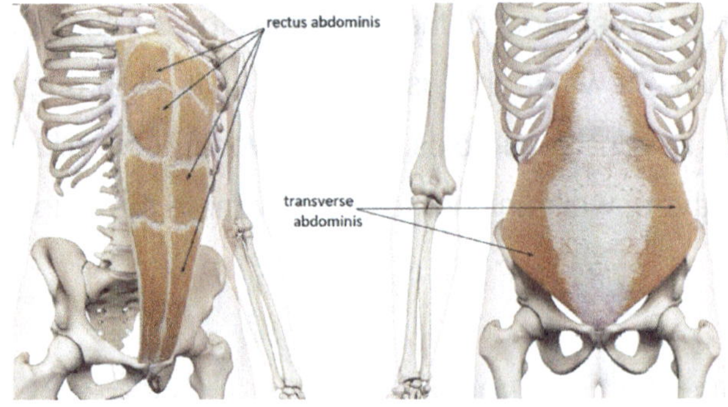

Figure 7.1 - Rectus abdominis and transverse abdominis muscles

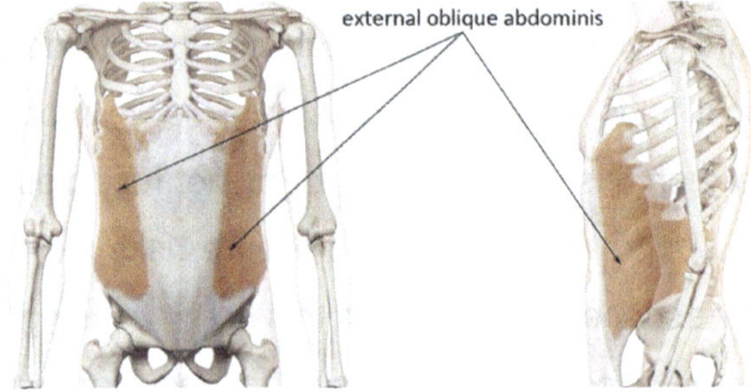

Figure 7.2 - External oblique abdominis

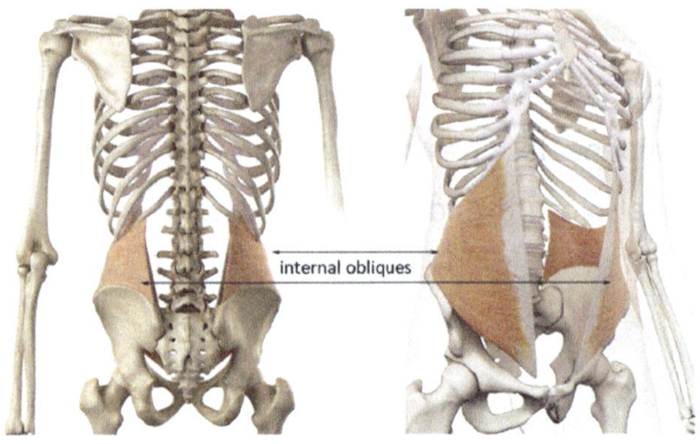

Figure 7.3 - Internal oblique abdominis

The abdominal muscles involved in exhalation exert pressure on the abdominal viscera, which in turn push the diaphragm back up toward its resting position. The internal intercostals are the opposite of the external intercostals; they reach from the lower rib to the one above, and work to pull the rib cage down and in. Muscles in the back (like the quadratus lumborum) also help decrease the size of the rib cage. But if all we did was contract the muscles of exhalation, air would simply rush out of us as fast as it could get through the vocal folds. To balance the action of those muscles, singers strive to keep the muscles of inhalation engaged as well. By working to maintain some space through the action of the inhalatory muscles, we can more precisely control the amount of air pressure that reaches the vocal folds. It is this muscular antagonism of the inhalatory muscles working against the expiratory muscles that generates the sensations of support.

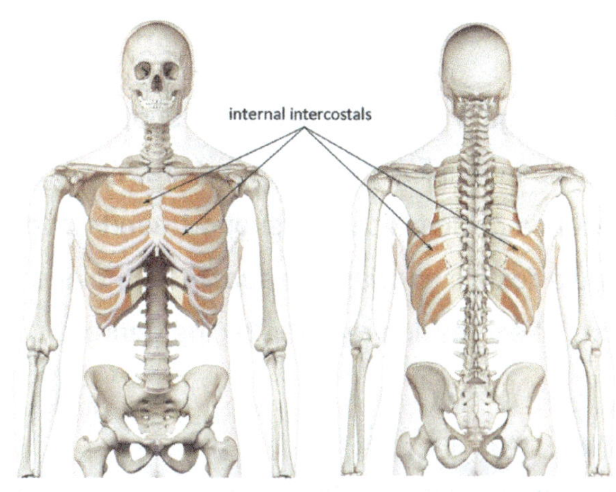

Figure 7.4 - Internal intercostal muscles

At its most basic level, the action of supporting the voice is about maintaining some expansion in the chest cavity while still exhaling. Keep in mind, it is impossible to stay completely expanded and still exhale: if there is no change in the space inside the body, there will be no air pressure change that initiates the outflow of air. Inward movement of the abdominal muscles and the rib cage is necessary, but that movement cannot go unchecked. Some singers choose to think about maintaining a slow and steady pace of inward movement. Others choose to allow one area of the body to move inward while another stays expanded. We typically recommend working to maintain expansion in the rib cage while allowing the abdominals to move inward, particularly for beginning students. But some singers find more success with maintaining outward pressure in the solar plexus, or by focusing on maintaining a high position of the chest. There are many ways to support the voice; choosing the correct strategy is about the constraints of the style at hand and the experience and individualities of the student in front of you.

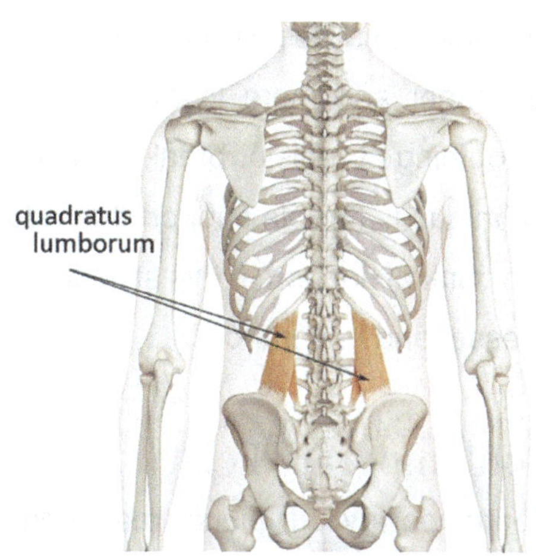

Figure 7.5 - Quadratus lumborum

The Art of Support

Many singers assume that more support is always better; however, with the short phrases in musical theater repertoire, the frequent use of the speech range, and the presence of amplification, support needs often are minimal. Musical theater singers need a flexible and variable support technique which serves all the styles, sounds, and types of expression required by the genre.

Traditional Legit

The traditional legit style is closest to the classical genre, so the type of support is like that of classical singing technique. The vocal folds are thinner in this style (more in Chapter 8), so less air pressure is required to set them in motion. This style often calls for longer and more legato lines, so support should be consistent and enduring. Smoothing of register breaks is also important in this style, and the foundation of that technique is flexible support that adapts to each register. Support is athletic, and you can think of support in this style like swimming—it requires strength, but also balance, finesse, and endurance.

Contemporary Legit

Contemporary legit pieces may require some of the same techniques as the traditional legit style, but they are often more speech driven with shorter phrases, less extreme ranges, and less concern for smooth register breaks. Less is more may be the key here; after setting up the inhalation, the singer may not need much more support than they use in speech. Of course, the demands vary with each piece, and perhaps even by phrase. Being well aligned, flexible, and ready to apply more or different support is always important. In general, support in this style can be as simple as taking a walk.

Traditional Belt

Belting is a different animal from legit singing and therefore requires more intense support. The vocal folds are thicker during belting, which results in high breath pressure and low breath flow. Creating and sustaining this high level of pressure requires that a singer engage their body differently. Many singers experience a sort of pushing out of the epigastrium (the area just below the sternum) during belting, while the abdominal muscles pull in. Try making a loud "shhh" sound and you'll likely experience the same sensation. Various types of anchoring may also be necessary, which we'll discuss later in the chapter. The traditional belt is like weightlifting not only because it requires strength, but also because it requires the proper technique to avoid injury.

Contemporary Belt

The contemporary belt style asks singers to produce varied vocal qualities, special vocal effects like runs or slides, and more extreme ranges while belting. These demands require the strong support of the traditional belt, combined with the flexibility and consistency of the traditional legit style of support. Anchoring is still important here, but higher and faster singing requires support that is both malleable and consistent, so changes at the vocal fold level are always matched with just the right amount of breath pressure. To close our metaphor, think of contemporary belt singing like gymnastics, as it requires both incredible strength and flexibility in equal measure.

The Art of Teaching Support
How can you talk about support with your students?

> *I find the lexicon of Bel Canto and Legit techniques to be an unintentional source of restricting behaviors for popular singers. These terms do not apply across all genres, as the timbres they encourage are not accepted in many sub-cultures of contemporary music.*
> *– Mark Baxter*[30]

As we mentioned at the top of this chapter, the concept of "support" goes by many names. Whether you call it "support" or "breath control" or "breath management," the most important thing is that your students understand what you are talking about and what you are asking them to do. A discussion of the science behind support can be helpful here. Not every student needs to know all the primary muscles of exhalation

---

[30] Benson, Elizabeth Ann. *Training Contemporary Commercial Singers.* Compton Publishing, 2020: 117.

by name or be able to explain Boyle's law (although some students thrive on that kind of information), but a basic understanding of the muscular antagonism between the inspiratory and expiratory muscles is appropriate in most cases. If you've already had a similar discussion about the mechanics of breathing, it's as simple as extending that conversation into exhalation territory. If your students can understand the muscular antagonism between the inspiratory and expiratory muscles—the "vocal struggle" (*lutte vocale*) as famed Italian pedagogue G.B. Lamperti called it—the sensations of support become less mystical and more replicable.

Training a singer to support, like every other area of vocal technique, requires that you help them cultivate a full and specific awareness of their body. Remember that because every human body is different, everyone's sensations are different. Prescribing a specific sensation of support to your students can lead to increased tension and effort, as they attempt to mold their bodies to your prescription. A more student centric path is to invite the student to observe and describe their sensations of support once you've identified that the sound is headed in the right direction. This invitation helps cultivate their bodily awareness while allowing you to acknowledge the individuality of the singer in front of you. Furthermore, using your student's language allows you to develop a shared vocabulary that likely has greater meaning to them than terms like "support" or "breath control."

That awareness becomes paramount as you help your student identify and develop a specific kind of support for each type of singing. Sensations of support will naturally differ based on the type of singing and level of intensity. Identifying and naming these support variations can help your students more effectively and quickly access the appropriate amount of support for the song, or even phrase, that they are working on. Using our athletic metaphor may be helpful, but it's always advisable to use your student's language.

It can be difficult for some students to develop awareness of support. In that case, suggesting some common sensations or sharing how you experience support can be useful in guiding their exploration. Singers often describe a sensation of leaning in the abdomen and chest, as if those muscles are leaning outward during singing. Others might choose a more vigorous word, like "push," although that sometimes has negative connotations for singing. It's important to offer multiple options, and stress that not all singers experience support in the same way. Teaching a singular manner of support can leave students struggling to fit a mold that doesn't work for them or feeling that their bodies and/or voices are inherently dysfunctional. As we discussed in Chapter 4, body image issues and other traumas can disconnect people from their bodies, so it is important that we provide gentle encouragement toward awareness, unconditional acceptance of our students' bodies, and a space that encourages our students to experience their bodies with agency and respect.

What techniques or exercises are useful?

Box breathing

Box breathing is an anxiety-reduction breathing technique, but, when done correctly, it can also be used to lay a foundation for support. The procedure is simple:

1. Inhale (breathe in) for four counts.
2. Suspend the breath for four counts.
3. Exhale (breathe out) for four counts.
4. Suspend the breath for four counts.

Combine this procedure with a focus on feeling inhalatory space, as we described in Chapter 5. Rather than instructing the student to breathe in or out, you might instead say "expand" and "collapse."

The most important part of this process is step 2: suspending the breath at the top of the breath cycle. When most of us hold our breath, we close the vocal folds to keep air from flowing out, but we can keep the air in our bodies without shutting the glottis. Remember that air pressure is directly related to the volume of our chest cavity; if the space we make during inhalation doesn't change, neither will the air pressure, and the air in our lungs will have no reason to go anywhere. In short, we can hold our breath just by maintaining our inhalatory space without closing the vocal folds.

You can teach your student to do this by asking them to hold their breath and observe the sensation in their throat. They'll likely feel some sort of pressure. Then, to eliminate that pressure, have them focus on maintaining their inhalatory space while imagining they're about to breathe out. Mentally preparing to breathe will keep the glottis open, and your student will be able to feel their throat stay open without air entering or exiting.

This exercise serves two purposes: first, it introduces the idea of maintaining inhalatory space, and gives the student a concrete way to feel the relationship between chest cavity volume and air flow. Second, it separates the function of maintaining inhalatory space from any sense of constriction in the throat so that the muscular work of support stays in the center of the body and doesn't travel up to the throat.

Unvoiced sounds

When you are first training support, it can be useful to focus solely on the support mechanism. Sustaining unvoiced fricatives, like a hiss or a "pshhh" sound, can help a student find and feel sensations of support without having to also focus on pitch or how they sound. These sounds also form an easy bridge to semi-occluded vocal tract exercises (see below), since they also create a valve at the front of the mouth.

Real-life parallels

Coughing and sneezing can often feel similar to effective support.[31] Try having your student put their hands on their rib cage and cough lightly. They'll feel a slight inward push of the abdominal muscles that can be paired with some expansion in the rib cage. Imagining a sneeze can do the same thing. Once the student feels the right action in the abdominal muscles, try substituting the cough or sneeze with the word "Hey!" But be careful to ensure that these ideas don't also induce constriction in the throat.

Semi-occluded vocal tract exercises

Semi-occluded vocal tract exercises (SOVTEs) are exercises that partially block air flow out of the vocal tract. Some common SOVTEs are lip trills, tongue trills, straw phonation, and singing on a /v/ or voiced /th/. Blocking the air flow creates a secondary valve, another point of resistance as the air leaves the body. Having a secondary valve reduces the amount of pressure at the primary valve, the vocal folds, which is why it's often easier to reach higher notes on a lip trill, or stay resonant on a tongue trill.

---

[31] Benson, Elizabeth Ann. *Training Contemporary Commercial Singers.* Compton Publishing, 2020: 113.

SOVTEs can function as instigators for the sensations of support. They also make it easy to experience how those sensations change in different ranges and intensities of sound. Higher pitches and greater intensities often require stronger support and moving through these areas on SOVTEs allows singers to experience the necessary increase in that "lean" feeling. But even as the sensation of support intensifies, SOVTEs always ensure air is still flowing. They are excellent tools for developing a sense of support.

SOVTEs create an immediate sense of balanced resistance in the intercostal, abdominal, and back muscles. We recommend combining these exercises with a focus on your student's bodily awareness, so they can identify and name their own sensations for each style of vocalization and in different registers. SOVTEs are also useful for learning to sustain legato lines and are therefore particularly effective for traditional legit style singing.

There are many ways to semi-occlude the vocal tract, and some may work better than others for different singers. You can choose which of these exercises to use with each student based on their needs and competencies, keeping in mind that not every exercise will be comfortable for every student. Be ready to switch them out if you find that a student has trouble rolling their r's or sustaining a lip trill.

Here are a few different SOVTEs:

- Lip trills
- Tongue trills (or rolled r's). These are particularly useful for singers who experience tongue tension, especially in the front of the tongue (more in Chapter 10).
- Raspberries (lip trills executed with the tongue out, vibrating between the lower lip and the tongue). These are also useful for those with tongue tension especially in the back of the tongue.
- Elongated "v" sound, like imitating a revving engine. These are easily combined with vowel sounds as a bridge from SOVTEs into regular phonation.
- Elongated voiced "th" sound, as in "they." This exercise functions very similarly to the "v," but it also pulls the tongue forward, which is useful for sufferers of tongue tension.

- Straw phonation (singing through a straw)
- "Buzzy oo" (imitating a straw, just using the lips). This exercise is particularly useful for accessing the treble upper range.

Straw phonation, deserves some special attention because while it can be incredibly useful for training efficient phonation, it only works if done correctly and with the correct straw. First, when your student is using a straw, make sure there is air coming through it; otherwise, the student is just humming around the straw with air coming through the nose.

Second, the straw is not a one-size-fits-all solution—literally. Some voice users will require a larger straw, others a smaller size. Smaller-diameter and longer straws offer more resistance, which means that more air pressure is pushing back on the vocal folds from above. Shorter and larger-diameter straws offer less resistance. When the diameter of the straw relates to the open/close phase of the vocal folds and the size and shape of the vocal tract, you get the most efficient outcome for your student's voice. Treble voices might need a slightly larger straw than modal voices because their vocal folds are smaller and resist less air. We are often matching the straw size to the resistance level (or closure) at the vocal folds: more closure means a thinner straw, less closure, a wider straw. Over time, you may find a smaller size works better as your student finds increased efficiency.

These sensations indicate the need for a larger-diameter straw:

- Squeezing
- Can't hit the high notes
- Head pressure (sort of like brain freeze)
- Squeezing in the throat

These sensations mean your student needs a smaller diameter:

- If it is too easy
- Lots of breath escaping

Try starting with plastic coffee straws and potentially sizing up to a larger stirrer or drinking straw. Or, if you are using plastic coffee straws, you can try using one, two or three straws together to achieve the best balance and feel.

SOVTEs in general offer you, the teacher, an excellent opportunity to hear what is going on at the vocal fold level without the camouflage of vowels and consonants. Breaks and other vocal inconsistencies in the SOVTE indicate inefficiency in vocal fold vibration, which often indicates an issue with the student's support. In this way, they're useful both as purely technical exercises and as ways of learning and preparing new music. We recommend having students sing through their pieces using one or multiple SOVTE exercises before using the words, so that both of you can closely observe their support in context.

Creating resistance

Giving the student something external to push against is often quite useful in developing support. Resistance bands, or exercise bands, are a popular tool, since they help engage the abdominal muscles. Use these by putting them around your student's forearms and having them maintain tension in the band while singing. Often anything that brings your student's attention away from their throat can help reduce tension, so any prop they can hold in their hands can be useful in this regard.

In the absence of props, you can (with your student's consent) use physical touch to help them achieve appropriate support. Instead of a resistance band, they can push their forearms out against yours, as you gently apply pressure inwards. Or you can place your hands on their ribs and apply gentle inward pressure, as you instruct them to keep your hands apart. Support is an athletic endeavor. Anything that helps your student engage their body beyond their throat is useful.

What pitfalls should I watch out for?

Avoiding locking

The big problem in teaching support is that students often misinterpret engagement of the abdominal muscles to mean static contraction. Support must always be dynamic and flexible. Locked support often results in excess tension in the throat, a strained tone, shaking in the head, jaw, or abdominal muscles, lack of vibrato, and sharp pitch.

The abdominal muscles should never be locked in position, but rather continually working in a direction. Take care to imbue your discussions of support with a sense of movement rather than stasis. When working with resistance bands, props, or gestures, always incorporate some movement. Walking while singing may also be helpful here.

Over- and under-supporting

Most students fall into one of two categories when it comes to support: overdoers and underdoers. Students whose tendency is to over-support often experience locking of either the intercostal muscles or the abdominal muscles. These students also often recruit the muscles of the throat in the support effort. For these students, a focus on release and relaxation can be helpful, as can combining support exercises with movement. Exercises that help increase the intensity of support may be detrimental for these students.

Underdoers tend to have difficulty consistently engaging their abdominal muscles. These students may experience excess tension in their throats or difficulty sustaining. Exercises that help these students feel more muscular engagement are necessary here, like working with resistance bands or physical tasks that require the abdominal muscles, like balancing activities. Exercises that focus on relaxation may be counterproductive.

The goal with every student is to help them find balance in every style and every register. Like so many aspects of singing, support is about finding the Goldilocks amount: not too much, and not too little. Understanding if your student tends toward too much or too little can help you guide them toward the middle.

The perils of switching

Often when a student's support is not serving them, it's because there's a mismatch between the style of support and the style of the music at hand. The support a singer needs for contemporary legit style singing and traditional belt style singing is necessarily different. Switching between styles, quickly and on command, can be quite difficult, and many musical theater songs require this feat, as the emotional arc of the song waxes and wanes. Codifying these styles of support, as we've advocated for throughout this chapter, may be occasionally tedious, but this is where it becomes useful. If your student is intimately familiar with their sensations of support in each style and register, even a single word can prompt them to correct their support and put them on track for the style at hand.

Support and the Flowchart

Support and Alignment

Since support is so reliant upon the body beyond the vocal tract, a singer's alignment can have profound effects on their support. As with breathing, being slumped over, with the sternum caved in and the shoulders pulled forward, can restrict a singer's ability to engage the inhalatory and exhalatory muscles. Being overly rigid is also problematic for support, as rigidity in other parts of the body can cause a student to lock the breath.

Conversely, finding a solid sense of support can help a singer find and maintain appropriate alignment. It's difficult to slouch if you're engaging your intercostal muscles; head and neck anchoring (see Chapter 8) assists in keeping the shoulders down and elongating the spine; anchoring in the torso by lifting out of the hips also helps to elongate the spine. More broadly, focusing on a flexible sense of support may help a student envision their alignment as dynamic rather than static.

Support and Breathing

Support is the extension of breathing: the expansion we find during inhalation is what our inhalatory muscles work to maintain during the "vocal struggle" that is support. The need for maintainable expansion is largely the reason why clavicular breathing doesn't work well. Whatever style of support the singer intends to use should inform the way they breathe, so they can find the position of the inhalatory muscles necessary to produce the right kind of muscular antagonism for the phrase and style at hand.

Not releasing that muscular antagonism at the end of the phrase can adversely impact the next breath. Keeping the muscles of exhalation engaged during inhalation restricts the body's ability to expand, which poorly impacts air intake and the singer's ability to support the next phrase properly. Many teachers refer to this phenomenon as "stacking tension," and it's easy to see how it can ripple out through an entire piece. Releasing the muscles of exhalation during inhalation is paramount and must be done without losing the position of the vocal tract or the overall sense of bodily engagement.

Support and Phonation

We discussed at the top of the chapter how phonation is reliant upon breath pressure to set the vocal folds in motion. But our ability to support is also reliant upon phonation, specifically our ability to maintain efficient closure of the glottis. If the singer cannot properly close the glottis, air will continue to rush through it regardless of how much or how little the singer engages their inhalatory and exhalatory musculature. Conversely, if the singer is prone to excess medial compression, the glottis will always require too much pressure to open and allow the folds to vibrate. This problem is often referred to as excess subglottal pressure, and it can be a precursor to vocal pathologies.

Efficient closure of the glottis is a prerequisite for efficient support, but thankfully, efficient support can help encourage efficient glottal closure. Students who are prone to excess medial compression have correctly intuited that their voice needs muscular engagement—they've just put it in the wrong place. For many students, the sensations of muscular engagement during support can serve as a substitute for their reliance on medial compression. Invite them to relocate their sense of engagement and control to a lower position in their bodies. Experiencing the "vocal struggle" in their inhalatory and exhalatory musculature can often help students experience less of a struggle in the throat.

Chapter 8: Registration

The Science of Registration

You must understand the source before you deal with the filter, meaning you must understand the function of the vocal folds before you understand how the throat and mouth act upon what happens.
– Jeanette LoVetri[32]

What is registration?

For our purposes, registration refers to the mechanisms by which we change the vibrations produced by the vocal folds, so that we can sing a variety of pitches at varying volumes. Vocal sound can be thought of as being affected by two parts: the source, or what vibrations the vocal folds are producing, and the filter, or how the shape of the vocal tract enhances or attenuates those vibrations. We'll talk more about the filter in the next chapter on resonance; registration is about what is occurring at the source, or in other words, how we move and alter our vocal folds.

Think of your vocal folds like a string on a guitar: thicker strings produce lower sounds, and thinner strings produce higher sounds. There are two sets of muscles that work together to allow a singer to thicken and thin their vocal folds to produce all the pitches in their range. These muscles are the thyroarytenoid (TA) and the cricothyroid (CT). The TA muscles form the body of the vocal folds (think back to the cover-body model from Chapter 6). Like flexing your biceps, this muscle shortens and thickens the vocal folds so that the singer can produce lower pitches. The TA muscle also assists in producing louder sounds, as thicker vocal folds stay closed

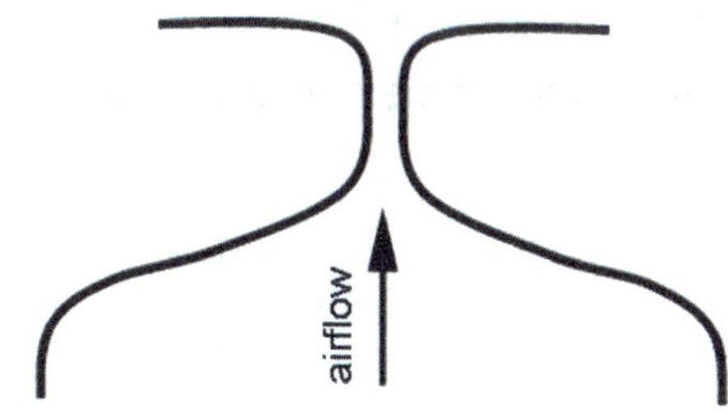

Figure 8.1 - Thick vocal folds, as during TA dominant phonation

Image presents a cross section of the glottis at the midpoint of the vocal folds

[32] Joan Melton. Singing in Musical Theatre: The training of singers and actors. Allworth Press, 2007: 47.

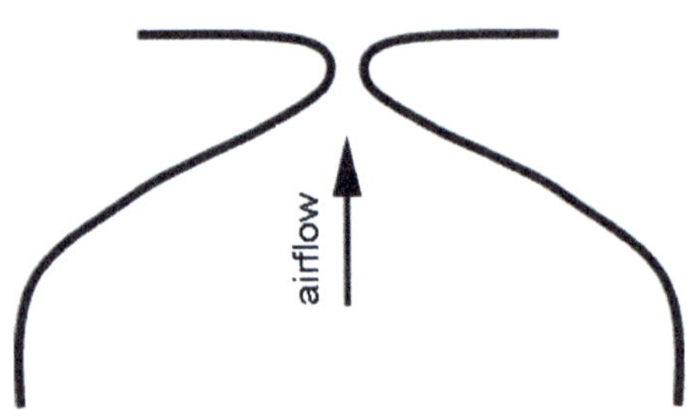

Figure 8.2 - Thin vocal folds, as during CT dominant phonation

longer (remember duty cycles from Chapter 6) and therefore produce stronger vibrations. The CT muscles do the opposite; they stretch from the cricoid cartilage to the thyroid cartilage on each side and tilt the thyroid cartilage away from the arytenoid cartilages. This action stretches and thins the vocal folds, allowing the singer to produce higher and quieter or lighter sounds.

Laryngeal position is also an important component of registration. As we discussed in Chapter 4, the larynx can move up and down within the neck. Remember that muscles that pull the larynx down (the infrahyoid muscles) help to tilt the thyroid cartilage forward, lengthening the vocal folds and encouraging head voice. Muscles that raise the larynx (the suprahyoid muscles) have the opposite effect. A lower larynx also helps create a warmer, loftier sound. Classical singing technique requires a "comfortably low" laryngeal position. A higher larynx contributes to a bright brassy timbre, as expected in belting. Moderation is key though; both low and high extremes of laryngeal position, produce undesirable sounds and are not sustainable in the long term.

What is a register?

Manuel Garcia, famed singing teacher of the 19th century, defined a vocal register as follows:

> *A register is a series of homogeneous sounds produced by one mechanism, differing essentially from another series of equally homogeneous sounds produced by another mechanism.*[33]

Fundamentally, that definition hasn't changed, but we now understand more about what exactly that "mechanism" might be.

[33] Manuel Garcia. *Hints on Singing*. London: E. Ascherberg, 1894.

Both the source and the filter define a register's specific mechanism, but the source (the function of the TA and CT muscles) is a large part of what gives any vocal register its distinct sound. Except at the very extremes of one's range, the TA and CT muscles are always working together. However, the balance between those two muscles shifts along a continuum, from extremely TA dominant at the lowest stretches of our range, to extremely CT dominant at the highest frequencies.

What happens between registers?

We all experience transition points in our voices; some of us call them "passaggios," others might use the work "break" or even "bridge."[34] Some singers experience many such areas of their range, where they feel a distinct shift. Others may only identify one or two. Whatever we call them and however many we sense in our own voices, these are the spots in our range where the "mechanism" of producing the sound changes.

Many of these shifts are acoustic in nature that arise due to the complex shape of the vocal tract and the way sound vibrates through it, and we'll discuss those more in the next chapter. But, the break we feel between chest voice and head voice (or full voice and falsetto, or TA dominant production and CT dominant production) is the result of a physiological shift in the larynx as the TA and CT muscles transfer power. The break or voice crack experienced by beginning singers—what one of our students once described as "that falling-up-stairs feeling"—is the result of an unstable laryngeal position during this transition. It takes incredibly fine motor control to do this smoothly, which is why it can take many years for a singer to successfully turn their "break" into a "bridge."

For all of us, modal and treble singers alike, this shift naturally occurs somewhere between C_4 and G_4. However, this point is not fixed; our break can be shifted up or down a considerable amount. There is a large portion of our middle voices wherein we can sing in chest voice or head voice depending on how we want to express ourselves. Even outside of the middle voice, no part of our range beyond its extremes is locked to one point on the TA to CT continuum. Registration is always a choice.

---

[34] Passaggio is the Italian word for passage and is often used in classical vocal pedagogy to describe register breaks.

One possible registration choice is the belt. The simplest description of belting is when a singer carries their chest voice, or TA dominant production, above their natural break, combined with an intense resonance quality. As the singer works to carry their chest voice beyond this point, careful attention must be paid to their breath support and their laryngeal position. When belting, a singer is asking their vocal folds to vibrate faster without slimming down as much. Thicker vocal folds require more air pressure to set them in motion, and faster vibration also requires greater air pressure. This increase in air pressure below the vocal folds is why belting is often characterized as a "low flow" mode of vocal production: comparatively little air is flowing through the vocal folds, as the thicker vocal folds help maintain high air pressure below them.

The correct laryngeal position for belting is a tight rope walk. Too low, and too much CT function is encouraged, so the tone loses its characteristic brassy quality. Too high, and the thyroid cartilage will lose its ability to tilt, restricting the singer's access to higher pitches and producing an overly pressed sound. Strategies for maintaining the right laryngeal position, often rely on both support and alignment and will be discussed later in this chapter. Strategies for teaching belting will be discussed in more detail in the next chapter, as this technique relies on principles of both registration and resonance.

Terminology

The terms 'belt' and 'legit' were coined especially to differentiate the heavier chest dominant singing style and the more 'classical' head register dominant sound. As this distinction proved to be far too general and limiting, the term 'mix' came into fashion with a vocal tessitura in the middle range (neither too high or too low). – Stephen Purdy[35]

Instead of imposing my terminology of chest, mix, head, on them, I ask them what they call the voice that they are using in a specific instance. Whatever terminology they are using, I will adapt to them.
– Wendy LeBorgne[36]

---

[35] Stephen Purdy. Musical Theatre Song: A Comprehensive Course in Selection, Preparation, and Presentation for the Modern Performer. Bloomsbury Publishing, 2016: 111-112.

[36] Elizabeth Ann Benson. *Training Contemporary Commercial Singers*. Compton Publishing, 2020: 126.

Registration is often regarded as one of the most complex areas of vocal pedagogy, but a good portion of that complexity stems from terminology. Many treble singers are familiar with the terms "chest voice" and "head voice"; many modal singers use "full voice" and "falsetto"; some teachers might use "Mode 1" and "Mode 2." These terms are all shorthand for TA dominant sounds and CT dominant sounds respectively. Many singers also use the term "mix" to describe a blending of these two registers. Physiologically, this term is inaccurate, as almost all the sounds we make involve both our TA and CT muscles. However, "mix" can be a useful term to describe the sensation of singing near the middle of that TA to CT continuum. We often use the terms "head dominant mix" or "head mix" to describe a fuller CT dominant sound, and the terms "chest dominant mix" or "chest mix" to describe a lighter TA dominant sound. If you think of registration as a continuum from 0 - 100, with 0 representing an all-TA sound, and 100 representing an all-CT sound, the chest mix exists around 40-50, and the head mix around 50-60.

Differences between terminology used for treble and modal voices can further complicate things. For example, "head voice" for modal singers has traditionally been used to describe a lighter TA dominant sound, or a chest mix, used in the upper range, while falsetto is used to describe a CT dominant sound. We prefer gender neutral terms that relate more to physiological function than voice type, so we often choose to use "chest mix" or "TA dominant mix" to describe this kind of phonation. "Speech-level singing," a term that has been coined by several well-known voice pedagogues, can also be useful to help singers maintain a speech-like quality in the head voice, and encourage a CT dominant mix.

Of course, as the above quote by Wendy LeBorgne describes, the best terms to use are the ones that mean something to your student. Provided you have a shared vocabulary, and your student can effectively communicate with the people around them about their singing, you can call registers whatever you want.

The Art of Registration

It is easiest to write about registration in black and white, but the truth is, there are many shades of gray. – Matthew Edwards[37]

In the course of a lifetime, human beings unknowingly make all the sounds required in singing. At play, when angry, when joyful, when in pain, nearly all combinations of head voice and chest voice, range, and volume are used to express the full range of human emotions. These changes in registration create colors and textures in the voice. Our human ability to vary the harmonic and emotional quality of a sung pitch also affects register variations. The harmonic content of a phrase directly affects the body's response to that harmony. In turn the pharynx, larynx, and muscles of breathing respond and the registration of the voice may subtly adjust. "The singer must be able to respond at will and with precision to the finest shades of musical, poetic and dramatic meaning."[38] The musical theater singer must be able to move from one style or registration to another seamlessly, as many roles contain songs which incorporate legit, belt, mix, and more registration styles.

Legit

This type of singing is heavily rooted in classical voice training and styles. It usually features many of the same distinguishing characteristics as classical/operatic singing, such as consistent vibrato, tall and round vowels, smooth register transitions, a balanced tone quality, "proper" diction, etc. The raised soft palate and lower laryngeal position create a darker quality. A lighter, more CT influenced coordination is common here, both for treble and modal voices. The differences between classical singing and the musical theater legit style stem mostly from resonance choices, like using brighter, more speech-like vowels than a classical singer would employ.

Traditional Belt

Belting is a speech-based vocal genre that requires incisive, percussive diction. It incorporates TA-dominant (chest voice) production for both treble and modal voices.

---

[37] Elizabeth Ann Benson. *Training Contemporary Commercial Singers*. Compton Publishing, 2020: 134.

[38] Thomas Hemsley. *Singing and Imagination*. Oxford University Press, 1998: 60.

The emotions expressed in belting are often extreme: joy, anger, exhilaration, etc. The use of chest register at a high pitch is likened to someone singing, yelling, rejoicing at the top of their voice. Chest voice used in this way is viscerally exciting for the listener, and it allows the singing-actor to express big emotions. But the belt voice must have a variety of loudness, weight, and the degree of openness of the vowel. This variability is an indicator of an efficient technique, which is essential in belting to prevent vocal injury (more on that in Chapter 11).

Contemporary

Contemporary musical theater created the need for registration that would allow the actor to sing even higher and brighter, expressing emotions in yet another way. This type of singing often combines characteristics of traditional musical theatre belt with contemporary pop/rock influences. It features bright, speech-based, sometimes straight-tone production, and frequently requires higher belting than traditional musical theatre singing. This feat is facilitated by nasal resonance and horizontal (as opposed to vertical, or tall) vowels. Pop and rock-type vocal ornamentation and embellishments are utilized at times, but the vocalism still has a decidedly musical theater sound. This style moves away from the use of head voice for treble voices and employs a higher range for modal voices. The modal singers favor high belting and lots of falsetto (CT dominance) whereas the treble singers favor lighter belting that can be carried higher into the "high belt," or belting above C_5.

Pop/Rock

This type of singing is an empathetic, reactive, and emotion-based genre of singing that embraces vocal distortions like growls, vocal fry, breathy tone, screams, glottal stops, and vowel manipulation (see Appendix, page 136, for a guide to some of these sounds). Treble and modal voices sometimes sing in similar ranges in this genre, and abrupt registration shifts are common. Smooth, legato singing and balanced registration is much less important. It is not unusual for stylistic authenticity to take precedence over text/lyrics, and there is often a heavy reliance on electronic amplification and instruments.

The Art of Teaching Registration

How can I talk to my students about registration?

Most students, even beginners, are aware of the "break" in their voices. Some might be self-conscious about it, others mystified by it, others determined to avoid it. It's often beneficial, especially for beginning students, to explain what's causing that breaking sensation physiologically. As always, we advocate for sharing the science, even in simple ways, to give students more agency in their singing and learning.

You'll often find students with an overdeveloped chest register and an underdeveloped head register. Most people use their chest register for speaking, and most modern music relies heavily on TA dominant sounds. For most people, head register is wildly under-utilized in daily life. Beginning students might find their head register foreign-feeling, weak, or difficult to access at all. More experienced musical theater singers might describe their head voice as disconnected from the rest of their voice, or as feeling inauthentic. But the head voice is essential, especially for singers who perform mostly with their chest voice. The flexibility that strengthened CT muscles provide is essential for expanding a singer's range, singing fast riffs and runs, achieving mix and high belt registers, and for staving off vocal injury. For the musical theater singer, access to a beautiful head voice sound opens doors to more styles, more timbres, and more ways to express. Understanding the importance of strengthening their head voice can encourage students to productively explore that part of their voice.

If you find a student who avoids a particular register or sound, it can be helpful to ask them what they're hearing. Remind them that what a singer hears in their head is not the same as what their audience hears (have you ever listened to your own voicemail message and immediately thought, "Do I really sound like that?"). Often the correct sound is unpleasant for the singer, at least at first. The hooty, rounded sounds of the traditional legit style might sound like operatic caricatures, or the bright, forward sounds of a belt might sound like obnoxious whining. In that case, invite them to direct their attention back to their physical sensations, while you take care of the listening. Remind them that they can trust you to help them make their best sound.

A final tip: sometimes students, even experienced singers, come to think of head and chest voice as a binary choice; in actuality, they exist on a sliding scale. You can invite students to explore this scale by thinking of their registration as a recipe that involves these two ingredients: head and chest voice. They can mix these two ingredients in varying ratios until they find the right feeling and sound. This kind of language encourages a sense of play and experimentation. Or you can explore the continuum metaphor we referenced earlier through color. Ask your student to give their head and chest voice sounds distinct colors. Blue is a common choice for head voice, and red is often used for chest voice. Then, you can describe the various sounds they're looking to make as different shades of purple.

What techniques or exercises are useful?

Many successful singers have learned to make sounds just by imitating what they hear. Providing students with good examples of different kinds of registration and inviting them to simply try to match those sounds can be a very efficient strategy for some singers. To that end, here are a few excellent examples of different kinds of registration in musical theater singing:

Traditional legit, treble voice:

- What's the Use of Wond'rin, from *Carousel,* sung by Shirley Jones
- Waitin' for my Dearie, from *Brigadoon,* sung by Marion Bell

Traditional legit, modal voice:

- The Impossible Dream, from *Man of La Mancha,* sung by Brian Stokes Mitchell
- Soliloquy, from *Carousel,* sung by Joshua Henry

Contemporary legit, treble voice:

- I Won't Mind, from *The Other Franklin,* sung by Audra McDonald
- Think of Me, from *The Phantom of the Opera,* sung by Sarah Brightman

Contemporary legit, modal voice:

- How I Am, from *Little Women*, sung by John Hickok
- Shouldn't I Be Less in Love with You, from *I Love You, You're Perfect, Now Change,* sung by Robert Roznowski

Chest Mix, treble voice:

- The Sacred Bird, from *Miss Saigon*, sung by Lea Salonga
- Better, from *Little Women*, sung by Sutton Foster

Traditional Belt, treble voice:

- When you're Good to Mama, from *Chicago,* sung by Queen Latifah
- Days of Plenty, from *Little Women*, sung by Maureen McGovern

Contemporary Belt, treble voice:

- No One Else, from *Natasha, Pierre, and the Great Comet*, sung by Philippa Soo
- Come To Your Senses, from *Tick, Tick…Boom*, sung by Alexandra Shipp

Traditional Belt, modal voice:

- Man, from *The Full Monty,* sung by Patrick Wilson
- Mr. Greed, from *The Life,* sung by Sam Harris

Contemporary Belt, modal voice:

- Waving Through a Window, from *Dear Evan Hansen*, sung by Ben Platt
- Larger Than Life, from *My Favorite Year*, sung by Evan Pappas

If a singer learns certain vocal coordinations through imitation, it's important to help them integrate these sounds and make them their own. Once they've found the appropriate sound, encourage them to identify their body's sensations and use those as the benchmark, rather than the imitated sound.

Different vowels, pitch patterns, imitations, and emotions can all instigate specific registration events. Cornelius Reid sums up the practical significance of specific vowels to registration as follows:

- "Ah" (/a/) requires more chest register participation than any other vowel and is easily activated, especially in the lower tonal areas, by singing or speaking at a loud volume with the mouth open.
- "Oo" (/u/) is head register dominated. Matching the texture of "Ah" to the "Oo" will reflexively decrease the domination of the chest register and incorporate more head register into the "Ah" (Oo-Ah). Conversely, with an excessively strong head register, the procedure should be reversed (Ah-Oo). Doing so should immediately supply more body and solidity to the tone.

- "Ee" (/i/) tends to coordinate the registration (as does "Ih"), but if resonated improperly through a dependence on mouth form, it will constrict the throat.[39]

Pitch patterns and melodic contour can also influence registration. Descending patterns can encourage singers to bring the lighter resonance of head voice down, whereas ascending patterns may induce excess weight into higher tones. Fast patterns encourage the CT muscles to assist in keeping the voice flexible.

Emotional cues can function as powerful catalysts for various registration events. The idea of whining often helps engage the CT muscles and lengthen the vocal folds. The sensation of calling out to a neighbor across the street in a friendly way invites more TA dominant function without constriction. Combining these two ideas, a whine and a call, can serve as an instigator for the belt sound.

The example exercises below explore these principles, but there are many more ways to help students experience the full variety of timbres and styles their voice has to offer.

Finding CT Dominance

- CT Dominant Speech

  Invite your student to imagine speaking softly to a sleeping baby or saying "aww" in response to a puppy or kitten. Often, students will naturally shift into CT dominant speech with these prompts.

- Hooting

  Imitate a foghorn, an owl's hoot, or the sound you achieve when you blow over a glass coke bottle partially filled with water. Try this technique in speech first, and then on single pitches in the CT dominant range, breathing between each pitch.

---

[39] Ariel Bybee and James E. Ford, eds.. *The Modern Singing Master: Essays in honor of Cornelius L. Reid.* Scarecrow Press, 2004: 141-142.

Finding TA Dominance

➢ TA Dominant Speech

Most people's speech is naturally TA dominant, so any speech will do! If you're looking for a fuller sound, try saying "Hey!" as if you're trying to get someone's attention, or "Go!" as if you're commanding someone to leave.

➢ "Zah"s

These clear, full-bodied, "engaged" sounds should be vigorous and loud, but not pressed or excessively "airy". Beginning with the "z" sound encourages air flow, so that the TA dominant "ah" vowel is not constricted or pressed.

Coordinating the Registers

➢ Yodels

Sing a hooty, head register dominated sound in the upper- middle range on "ooh", and then yodel or "crack" down to a chest register sound the octave below on "ah". In the same breath, return to the upper-octave pitch on the "ah" vowel, this time with a blended sound and without the yodel.

➢ Slides or Sirens

On any vowel, start on a low pitch to ensure the TA is involved, and slide up to the top of the range to encourage it to coordinate with the CT. This will train a mixed voice quickly. If you have a crack in the middle, singing through a straw regularly will smooth that out over time. Siren from the top down as well. Start on the highest comfortable pitch and glide down to the very bottom.

➢ Laughing

Laugh down from the top of the range. Go as fast as you can, but keep it natural, like a giggle. Repeat with an SOVTE (a straw is particularly useful here). Once you're used to it on the SOVTE exercise, take it on an arpeggio up and down the range. Speed, without sacrificing clarity and separation of each giggle, is one of the goals of this exercise.

- Messa di voce

  Messa di voce is a technique borrowed from classical singing where the singer executes a crescendo and then decrescendo while sustaining a single pitch. Since our vocal folds thicken for loud sounds and thin out for softer sounds, this is really an exercise in registration. Messa di voce is a difficult exercise that requires fine motor control, so consider using this technique with more advanced singers. Try using the sequence "ooh, you, ah, you, ooh" with this exercise, so that "ooh" is for your softest sounds, "you" for the medium sounds, and "ah" for the loudest sounds.[40]

Emotional impetus

As with every area of musical theater technique, registration must always be connected to emotion. To assign an emotional context is to assist the student in effectively achieving the level of support that they require. Jo Estill often uses the expression of the "joyful shout" to describe belting. Exhilaration is a useful emotional prompt that assists in finding a vocal posture that is both engaged and open, and there are many more:

- A joyful call, like saying hello to a friend across a crowded room or across the street, for heightened speech-level support.
- Whining, like a puppy whimpering at a closed door, or a child saying, "I don't wanna," for greater CT involvement.
- Being assertive for more TA involvement, like saying "never never never never, no!"

We encourage you to help your students play with these emotions and exercises! Let them imagine scenarios where they might joyfully shout, or call out to a friend, or whine, or emphatically refuse! As you and your student explore repertoire, make note of any specific emotions or narratives that help your singer access specific sounds to use as prompts in future practice.

---

[40] Norman Spivey and Mary Saunders Barton. *Cross Training in the Voice Studio: A balancing act.* Plural Publishing, 2018: 50.

What pitfalls should I watch out for?

Register imbalance usually results in undesirable muscular tension in the intrinsic and extrinsic laryngeal muscles and the various muscles of breathing. This excess tension can be the cause of vocal pathology, if sustained over a long period of time, as it puts more pressure on the vocal folds as they vibrate against each other. We'll discuss vocal health further in Chapter 11 but suffice it to say that any signs of excess muscular tension should be addressed promptly by bringing a student's registers back into balance.

Although belting (which we'll discuss more in the next chapter) often garners the most attention, a "mixed" sound is the foundation of most musical theater singing. Until a student can achieve an efficient mixed sound, we advise staying away from belting. Developing a flexible mix can be difficult, as it induces constriction for many singers. But with some practice, it becomes possible to move from the chest voice to the head voice while maintaining "speech-level singing." To achieve this goal, the chest voice must be flexible and light, without too much dynamic loudness. Then, it is helpful to use a slightly whiny quality— like a little cry, or a puppy's whimper—to allow the vocal folds to stretch. Using ascending patterns (like scales and arpeggios) starting in the lower range gives your student the opportunity to practice releasing some of the chest voice as they move along the registration continuum toward head voice for the upper notes. When devising exercises to teach the "mixed" sound, it is helpful to remember Cornelius Reid's qualification of the vowels: "ah" is the chest register dominant vowel and "oo" is the head register dominant vowel.

Registration and the Flowchart

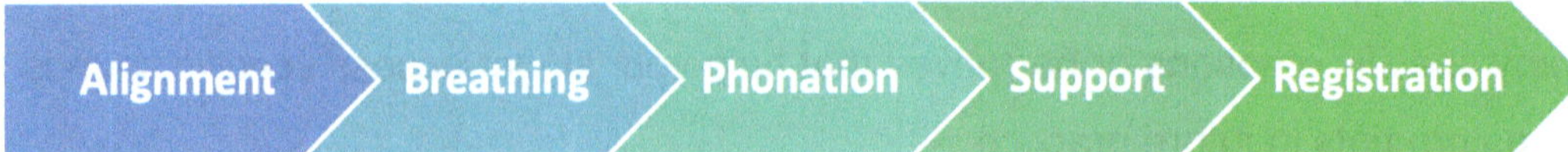

Alignment and Support: Anchoring/Grounding

Much of the athletic singing in musical theater requires additional techniques of supporting the larynx to maintain its optimal position within the neck. This recruitment of additional muscles in the body and larynx ensures stabilization of the larynx and improved resonance. Some of the terms used for this additional type of support are "anchoring" and "grounding," and they allow singers to create louder sounds sustainably. These sounds must be "embodied" through grounding techniques.

Grounding the Head and Neck:

1. Extend the top of the skull to the ceiling, keeping the neck in line with the spine. Feel the lengthening of the neck.
2. Place the palm of your hand on the back of the skull. Press the skull gently into your hand.
3. Practice steps 1 and 2 while singing any vowels on some easy pitches. Be sure that the knees are not locked. Compare this to singing *without* using steps 1 and 2 and notice increased feelings of support.

Grounding the Pharynx:

It's also necessary to create a firmer stretched feeling in the oral and nasopharynx for athletic singing (like belting) to increase resonance. Grounding the nasal and oral pharynx with a feeling of width and height, stretching of the soft palate, can be achieved using the following steps:

1. Breathe through your nose as if smelling something like a freshly baked cinnamon bun or some beautiful flowers or the fresh ocean air. The nostrils widen and there is a firm but elastic stretch in the soft palate and the throat. Practice maintaining this feeling without making funny faces or doing strange things with the eyes.
2. Think about concealing a yawn when you don't want to be rude, when you are tired or really bored in the company of others.

Grounding the Chest:

1. Standing comfortably with feet apart and soft knees, turn your arms in their sockets away from the body.

2. Bend your elbows slightly and imagine that there are semi-soft balls (like tennis balls or stress balls) under your armpits.
3. As you sing, squeeze these imaginary balls so that you are pulling the elbows down and in toward the body.[41]

Breathing

As we've alluded to previously, one's method of inhalation has an impact on laryngeal position through a phenomenon known as tracheal pull. Remember that your diaphragm is connected to your lower six ribs on each side; your rib cage is connected to your lungs via pleural linkage; the bronchi in your lungs are connected to your trachea; and your trachea is connected to your larynx. This series of connections means that all these parts move together to a certain degree. As the diaphragm fully descends, it pulls everything down with it just slightly, including the larynx. This arrangement is ideal for legit or classical singing, as a low, full breath helps bring the larynx down to the slightly lower position you want for those genres. For belting however, the tracheal pull means that a low breath may be working against the singer. Aiming for lateral expansion in the rib cage, rather than vertical expansion in the abdomen, is necessary for belting. "Breathe into your armpits" may be a helpful prompt.

Phonation

Directly above the (true) vocal folds are your ventricular folds, or false vocal folds. These extra folds aren't normally involved in phonation, but they are responsible for the popping sound of vocal fry. Sometimes singers recruit them for growling sounds in rock or heavy metal. However, unnecessary constriction in the throat can bring them together accidentally, which creates excess noise in tone, or even blocks the sound altogether. This issue is a particular concern when belting, as the extra exertion required sometimes results in a tendency to squeeze the throat. Retraction is the active effort to abduct the false vocal folds, and it can be achieved with a bit of practice with these three exercises:

---

[41] Gillyanne Kayes. *Singing and the Actor.* Routledge, 2004: 81.

1. Think about the urge to sneeze. The very beginning of the sneeze creates a feeling of width in the pharynx.
2. Think about the urge to laugh when it is not appropriate to do so: the "contained" laugh.
3. Inhale and exhale making absolutely no noise. Silent breathing is an indication of abducted false vocal folds.[42]

Practice these to achieve false vocal fold abduction upon the inhalation in preparation to sing.

---

[42] Ibid., 11.

Chapter 9: Resonance

The Science of Resonance

What is resonance?

Up until this point, we've been discussing anatomy and physiology. In this chapter, our scientific discussion shifts to acoustics and the laws of sound. Last chapter we talked about the source-filter theory of voice production, and how registration alters the source of our sound. Resonance is about the filter, or how the vocal tract—from the vocal folds all the way up to the mouth—alters the original vibrations of the vocal folds to produce a specific timbre.

The sound that comes out of the vocal folds is a complex sound, meaning it has more than just one pitch. The pitch we hear is called the fundamental frequency, and it is the lowest and loudest frequency produced. But other frequencies, sometimes called overtones or harmonics, are also produced, and our brains interpret all of these other frequencies and their relative strengths and weaknesses as the timbre of a sound. The original sound that leaves the vocal folds has what we call *spectral slope* (Figure 9.1), meaning that the strength of each subsequent overtone drops off at the same rate. However, a sound that has passed through the vocal tract looks more like this (Figure 9.2):

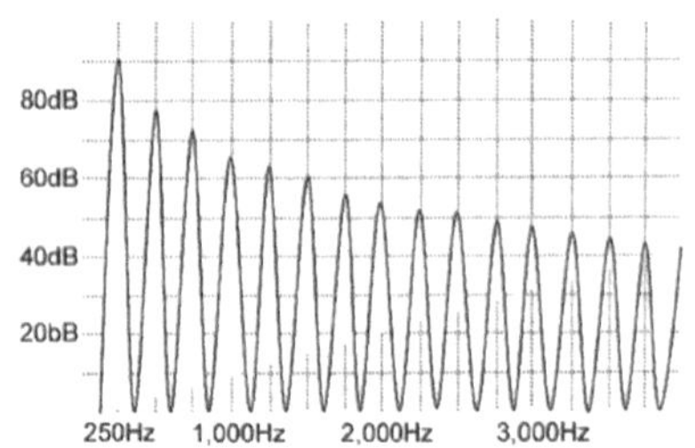

Figure 9.1 - Spectral slope

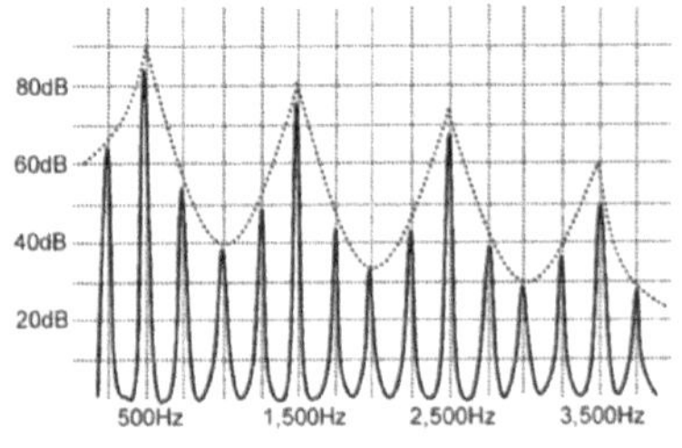

Figure 9.2 - Spectral envelope

Notice how certain overtones are enhanced and do not drop off at the same rate as the spectral slope. This frequency distribution is called the spectral envelope, and it is this shape that translates into timbre.

How do we change our timbre?

The short answer to this question is that the vocal tract is made up of soft, malleable tissues that can change shape. The vocal tract includes all the structures above the vocal folds: the pharynx, mouth, and nasal cavity. Imagine the bell of a trumpet: if you dented it, wouldn't the trumpet sound different? The same is true of our voices; we change our timbre by changing the shape of our vocal tract.

The long answer for how we turn spectral slope into spectral envelope has to do with an acoustic phenomenon known as a formant. A formant (also called a resonance) is a resonant frequency of the vocal tract. A resonant frequency is a frequency at which a space naturally vibrates with greater intensity. The vocal tract has multiple pockets that have their own resonant frequencies, or formants. Think of formants like a filter that you might apply to a photo; the filter stands ready to enhance certain colors already present within the picture and downplay others. Formants enhance frequencies within their range, and attenuate those beyond them. Those frequencies can be the fundamental frequency or any of the overtones the vocal folds produce.

Because the vocal tract is full of soft tissue, those spaces that create formants can change shape. This means the frequencies each formant amplifies change as we change the shape of our vocal tract. These changes, subconscious or not, are accomplished by movements of the tongue, jaw, soft palate, pharyngeal constrictors, and laryngeal elevators and depressors (more on those in Chapter 10).

By changing the frequencies our formants enhance, we can strategically align the formants with the frequencies the vocal folds produce. This interaction of frequencies and formants explains why certain vowels might work better in different parts of a singer's range. The pitch the singer is trying to sing, or its overtones, can be aligned with the formant frequencies produced by a specific tongue position, mouth position, or other overall arrangements of the vocal tract.

Of course, since the vocal tract is just a filter, some of our timbre is dependent upon the sound coming from the larynx. The thicker the vocal folds, the stronger the overtones are. To put it another way, a more TA dominant sound will have a shallow spectral slope, whereas a more CT dominant sound will have a steeper spectral slope as the strength of the overtones drops off more quickly.

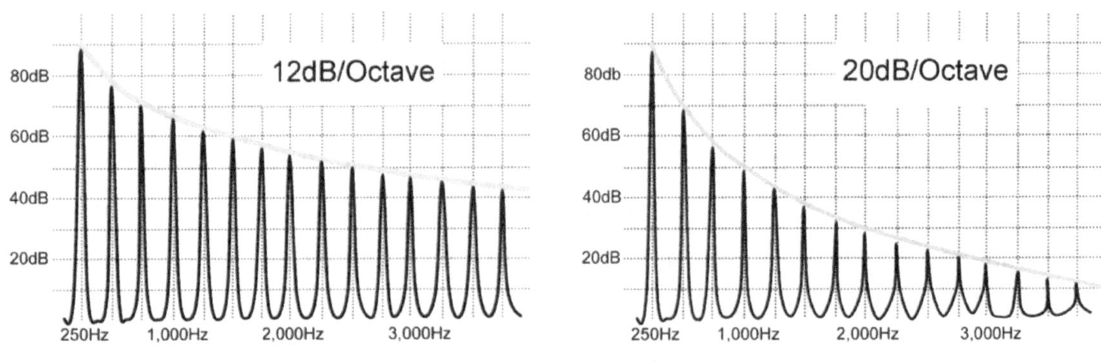

Figure 9.3 - Shallow spectral slope, as in a more TA dominant sound, and steep spectral slope, as in a more CT dominant sound

Think of the picture analogy: a photo filter that picks up blues and greens will have a different effect on a picture of an ocean than one of a desert. The shape of the vocal tract can only alter the sound created at the vocal fold level to a certain extent.

What and where are the formants?

The first and second formants are largely defined by tongue position and therefore change based on the vowel a singer is producing. Reducing space in the front of the vocal tract with a high tongue vowel, like "ee", lowers the frequencies amplified by the first formant and raises those of the second. Reducing space in the back of the vocal tract lowers the frequency of the second formant, as in the "ooh" vowel. Opening the mouth also raises the first formant, as for an "ah" sound. This chart plots each vowel based on the frequency ranges of the first and second formant.

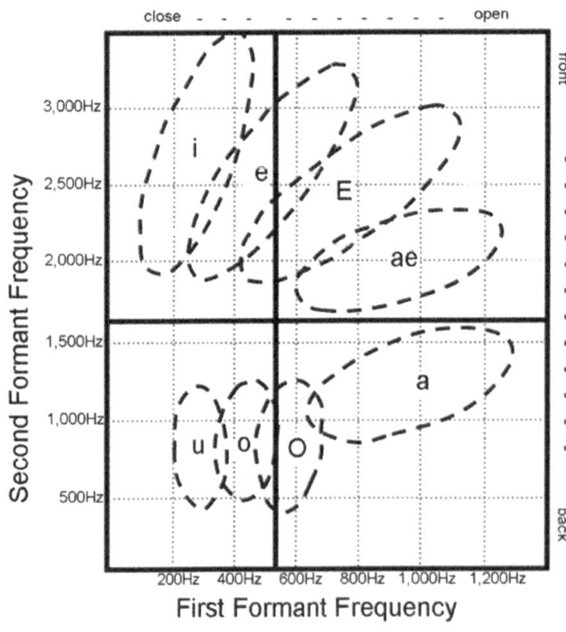

Figure 9.4 - Vowel chart

Remember that vowels aren't just mouth or even tongue positions.

The shape of the whole pharynx influences those formant frequencies and the sound of our vowels.

The third, fourth, and fifth formants, sometimes collectively called the singer's formant, are generated by spaces deeper in the vocal tract, and are therefore not affected by tongue position and do not change based on the vowel. The singer's formant amplifies frequencies between 2800 Hz and 3400 Hz and is the reason an operatic voice can carry over an orchestra, or a baby's cry can be heard across a crowded room. Physiologically, a stronger singer's formant comes from a narrowing of the aryepiglottic sphincter (AES) When this narrowing of the AES is combined with a higher larynx, lowered soft-palate, arched tongue position, and horizontal vowel shape, you get what many people refer to as twang. Adding twang, particularly when belting, adds a ringing quality to the voice and reduces strain. We'll discuss stylistically appropriate uses of twang and how to help your students develop it, but for now it's important to note that twang utilizes the singer's formant to achieve a louder sound that carries better.

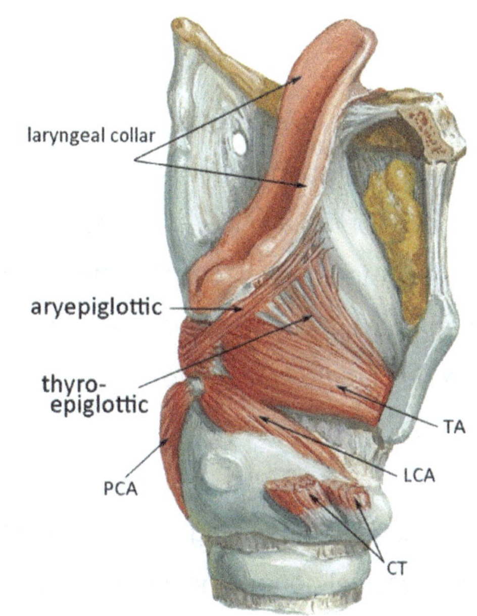

Figure 9.5 - Aryepiglottic sphincter

Netter medical illustration used with permission of Elsevier.

In the last chapter, we alluded to register shifts that arise from acoustic shifts, rather than the physiological shift felt at the transition point between TA dominance and CT dominance. These shifts occur when the frequencies of the pitch and its overtones align differently with the formant frequencies of the vocal tract than in other areas of the voice. Voice teachers often recommend different versions of vowel modification in these areas of the voice—like opening or closing the vowel more than one would in speech. Those vowel modifications are designed so the current pitch and its overtones are better aligned with the frequencies of the first and second formants. This strategy is one way voice teachers help their students manipulate and maintain the correct timbre, or in scientific terms, the correct spectral envelope.

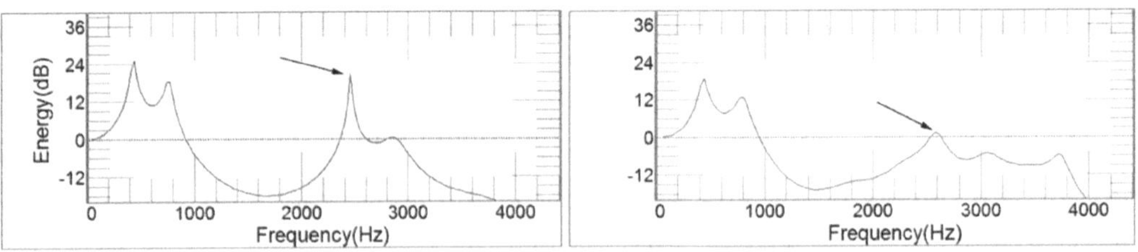

Figure 9.6 - Aligned and then misaligned formants

The Art of Resonance

The myriad ways in which we can position our vocal tract, combined with the various versions of sounds our vocal folds alone can produce, result in a whole rainbow of vocal colors at a singer's disposal. The musical theater genre takes advantage of that flexibility to enrich each character's life and create a specific "vocal identity." In musical theater singing, all types of speech and singing sounds are necessary: speech quality, mix, legit, belt, twang, etc.

Traditional Legit

Traditional legit singing employs a warmer, fuller kind of resonance that is closest to the classical genre. The words still come first (that's what separates this style from the classical genre) but a unified, smooth tone is more important here than in other styles of musical theater. Generally, vowels are slightly rounded and tall, and vowel modification can be employed more liberally to maintain a consistent tone from top to bottom.

Contemporary Legit

Contemporary legit styles are speech-based, so generally we avoid too much loft in the sound and strive for a conversational timbre that matches the speaking voice. Bright, clear, forward, and ping-y are all useful words to describe this sound. Vowel modification, should only be employed as is technically necessary; it's paramount that the words be heard and understood consistently.

Belt

Belting requires, by definition, a bright and brassy sound. Twang can come into play here, rarely as a main characteristic of the sound, but often as an essential ingredient in maintaining TA dominant production and/or a clear mixed sound. Vowel modification can be part of that effort too, particularly toward more forward and open vowels like "ah" (as in father) or "aeh" (as in cat).

Rock/Pop and Other Genres

There are lots of shows that don't quite fit into these traditional resonance camps because of the influence of commercial music genres. In these instances, the sound should be a blend of that traditional musical theater sound and the sound of the other influential genre(s). A rock-influenced show might require more vowel modification to match the emotion-filled, rough sound of rock and roll. R&B might mean adding more depth and fullness to the sound, while country could mean more twang. And always be ready for vocal distortions like growls, vocal fry, breathy tone, screams, and glottal stops (see Appendix, page 136). But in any style, it's important for you and your student to listen to lots of different artists and interpretations to go beyond describing the sound to really understanding the conventions of the style.

Beyond Style

A few factors influence what type of sound or timbre a singer chooses—and it should always be a choice. The first is the specific genre or style at hand. But even a perfect conception of stylistic conventions will only get a singer so far. The second factor necessary for choosing their sound is the emotional content of the song. In any style, it's rare to find a belted lullaby. A smooth, lofty tone doesn't lend itself to expressing rage. Remember, musical theater singing is never just about tone, it's about how that tone conveys the feelings of the character.

Finally, and most crucially, the singer brings their unique perspective to this character choice. They are the vessel for the character, and so each character is slightly different from singer to singer, as it changes shape to fill each unique vessel. There are of course industry conventions (for example, it's rare to hear "Defying gravity" sung in a legit style), but sometimes rules are made to be broken. The character and the emotion are paramount; if they connect with the audience, little else matters.

The Art of Teaching Resonance

How can you talk to your students about resonance?

Keep it simple! Take the following explanation as an example of the kind of conversation you might have with a student—one that doesn't leave out the science, but also doesn't make things overly complicated.

Generally speaking, there are two types of resonance:

1. *Primary resonance,* which is generated in the larynx, regardless of the speech-sound intended.
2. *Secondary resonance* which modifies the larynx-generated sound for a specific speech-sound (vowel shape).

Primary resonance, is always available to the singer. This resonance occurs at the laryngeal level and is present from the very first moment of phonation. Secondary resonance is dependent on what the singer wants to say, both in a literal and emotional sense. As soon as breath meets the vocal folds, the vibrations that occur resound off the nearest sounding boards. The nature of vibrations is to multiply as they travel through the spaces of the pharynx, mouth, nose, the bony structure of the chest, the cheekbones, the jawbone, the sinuses, the skull, and the cartilages of the larynx, all of which contribute to resonance. Resonance work, and vowel work, is often about matching the primary and secondary resonances together, and with the emotion at hand, to make sure that those vibrations have the best possible structure in which to bounce around.

Formants, frequencies, and the science of acoustics can be a daunting subject even for advanced singers (speaking from our own experience!). What's important for singers to understand is the broader idea of source and filter, or primary and secondary resonances, and how they can work to align them.

Working on resonance also provides a great opportunity to explore and develop your student's creativity. Invite your student to play with the different sounds they can make. They can mimic sounds, take things to extremes, and explore every possible option at their disposal. Color is an apt metaphor for vocal quality; imagine every new timbre as a new paint on your student's palette, each one providing more depth and originality to their work.

One popular way to discuss resonance is through the concept of "placement," however, we advise against this approach. The idea of "placement" divorces the sensations of resonance from the mechanisms that created them, like efficient phonation, active support, and appropriate registration. It also, at the very least semantically, disconnects the voice from the body by creating the idea that the entire voice can be picked up and moved to various spots in the student's face, head, or chest. The hope in a "placement" approach is that some reverse engineering will occur—that manufacturing the ideal sensations of resonance will bring all the other vocal systems into line—but we've often found that directions like "place the sound behind your eyes" very quickly lead to constrictions as the student tries to forcibly put their voice in a certain spot and hold it there. The result is a cheap facsimile of a student's best singing, along with confusion and frustration when fixing their "placement" doesn't fix their problem.

One final problem with the concept of "placement" is that it prescribes specific feelings, rather than allowing your student to explore the uniqueness of their body, their instrument, and their experience. Asking your student, "where do you feel vibrations in your body?" can help you better understand what is happening in their mechanism. More importantly, it helps your student develop their internal senses. Help your student make connections between the way they move their vocal tract and the way they feel their voice vibrating in their body—their *whole* body. Feeling their instrument in its entirety with specificity and precision will lead to refined, colorful, and connected singing.

What techniques and exercises are helpful?

Discovering sensations of resonance

Awareness is, as always, the first step. For many beginning students, the idea of a sound that is more forward or back, more closed or open, is a foreign concept. Before you can direct them, you must help them become aware of their sensations of resonance. Chest resonance is an easy place to begin your exploration: have your student put their hand on their chest and call out in their speaking voice. They'll very likely feel their chest vibrating. From there, have them do a siren and ask where those vibrations travel to help them discover head resonance.

To find forward and back sensations, you can start with a spoken "ah" and have them bring the sound into their nose. Then go the other way: have them direct their sound into their throat. Play with these sounds, find all the gradations in between, and ask a lot of questions! Some students might describe these feelings with literal specificity, some might use metaphors, some might even use colors! Whatever language your student uses to describe their experience is the most effective language to guide them in the future.

"Ng" sounds

Try holding an "ng" sound, like the end of the word "sing," and notice what you feel in the back of your mouth. You should find that your soft palate lowers and touches the back of your tongue as all your air is directed through the nose. Utilizing this sound, particularly in combination with a vowel in exercises like "hung-ah" can help a student become aware of the movement of their soft palate. The "ng" sound is also useful for discovering forward sensations of resonance, and can serve as an introduction to the twang sound. Be wary of excess tension in this sound, as some singers tend to push or drive through this kind of nasal tone. But if it is freely produced, the "ng" can be a very helpful tool.

Medializing

The differences in each vowel's first and second formant values means that, for many beginning singers, there are big differences in the way vowels sound. How often have you found that an exercise that works on an "ee" vowel falls apart on "ah"? Or that a sudden "oo" vowel in the text changes the sound entirely? The singer's challenge is to make all their vowels similar enough that the sound doesn't change but keep the words intelligible. Medializing is one strategy for this issue, and it works by bringing the hump of the tongue forward and making the necessary tongue position adjustments in the middle of the mouth, rather than the back.[43]

Diagram 16: [uː] *as in 'shoes'*

Diagram 17: medialised [uː]

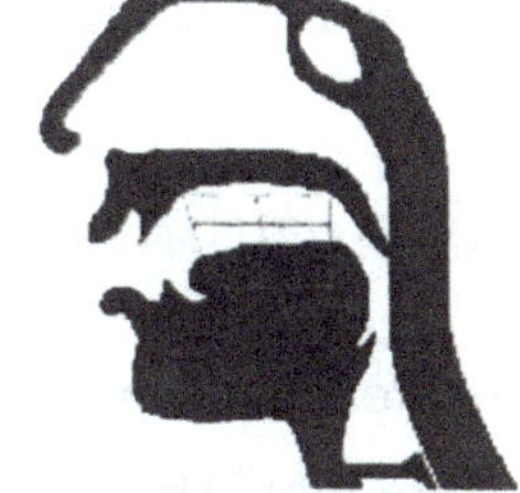

Diagram 18: [ɔː] *as in 'horse'*

Diagram 19: medialised [ɔː]

Diagram 20: [ɒ] *as in 'soft'*

Diagram 21: medialised [ɒ]

Figure 9.7 – Medialised [sic] *vowels, taken from Singing and the Actor by Gillyanne Kayes, see citation*

Finding twang

We often say to our students, "the road to beautiful singing is paved with lots of ugly noises." Nowhere is this truer than in developing twang. Twang can be used in any range of the voice but in contemporary musical theater, it is utilized most often in the upper range. It can have either chest voice or head voice as its foundation. You'll need

[43] Gillyanne Kayes. *Singing and the Actor*. Routledge, 2015: 103.

to start with noises like a bratty kid saying "nyaeh nyaeh nyaeh," a cat yowling, or a witch's cackle—the uglier the better. It can be a challenge for beginning, or even intermediate students to feel comfortable making these sounds: be ready to demonstrate and allow yourself to be silly.

When produced with enough ugliness, these noises should have an incredible amount of ring, or carrying power. Once your student can achieve that in noise, start adding pitch. Help them avoid the urge to make the sound pretty; think of making sounds on pitch, not "singing." From there, open these sounds to a vowel like "ae" (as in hat) or "ee," and keep working to maintain ring in the sound.

What pitfalls should I watch out for?

As we've stated, the musical theater genre makes use of all kinds of sounds and timbres that the human voice can produce. There are, however, some extreme sounds that are not viable for performance. Some singers who stray too far to one side of the spectrum just have a natural proclivity toward a certain kind of resonance that their teacher must carefully help them balance. Others may have developed that habit as a reaction against some perceived deficit in their singing, acting on advice—like "sing into your mask" or "open your mouth"—that was taken out of context or too liberally applied.

When a sound is too bright, you're dealing with a lack of space in the vocal tract due to the contraction of the constrictor muscles and elevation of the larynx. The idea of starting a yawn can help the student find some more lift in their soft palate and relaxation in the throat. Exercises to find more freedom in the jaw and tongue may also be helpful; we'll address those in the next chapter. Usually, singers with an overly bright sound feel concentrated vibrations in their face, particularly around the mouth. See if they can find a broader base for those vibrations in the center of the body and in the chest, to add depth both to the sound and to their sensations.

Sounds that are too dark are often caused by excess tension in the yawning muscles: a depressed larynx, pharyngeal walls that are too flabby, overly lifted soft palate, and a pulled-back tongue. But an overly dark sound can also come from too little energy or direction in the tone and in their sensations of resonance. Take care to correctly identify the cause of a student's darkness; a student whose issue is excess tension will be ill-served by an approach that focuses on adding more energy, just like a student who lacks momentum won't benefit from a focus on relaxation. Dark and breathy often go hand and hand. The darkness will disappear when the breathiness is eliminated.

People disagree on how much nasal resonance can or should be used in musical theater singing. Some singers and teachers never allow nasality, others bring it in occasionally, particularly in pop and pop-influenced styles. Some nasality may be helpful for some students, particularly in navigating the passaggio. However, too much will result in an unpleasant sound that loses carrying power. Additionally, nasality does not readily reveal the emotional life of a character. Hypernasality occurs when the nasal port is not sufficiently closed by the elevated soft palate, and too much air flows through the nasal cavity. An inactive palatal muscle and incorrect tonal models are usually the culprits. You can use a flashlight to show the student what an elevated palate looks like, and they can practice lifting their soft palate in the mirror. The use of [g] or [k] as in "gah" and "kah" is also helpful. Imitating loftier sounds may help your student develop a new tonal model. As always, direct them toward their internal sensations. Hyper-nasal sounds, like overly bright sounds, often result in a concentration of vibration at the front of the face; a broader base for those sensations can help. Watch out for excessive tension in the pharynx. Constriction, particularly the type that results in a lack of oral space can be a cause of this problem.

Resonance and the Flowchart

Alignment > Breathing > Phonation > Support > Registration > Resonance

Resonance and Alignment

The alignment of our entire body affects everything we do as singers, but when thinking about its effect on resonance, the position of the neck and head is particularly important. Try this experiment: choose a comfortable pitch and vowel and hold the note while tilting your head all the way back. Try not to make any adjustments, just notice what changes you hear and feel as you compress the back of your neck. The neck essentially houses and provides structure for the vocal tract; if that structure is compromised on the outside, it's difficult to make the right adjustments on the inside. If a student is struggling to maintain consistent resonance, take a glance at the position of their head and neck.

Resonance and Breathing

Put most simply, manipulating our resonance is about shaping our vocal tract to change the way the air leaving our bodies vibrates. But what about when air enters our bodies? Obviously, there's no sound to resonate during inhalation, but the position of the vocal tract still matters. By remembering the specific sensation of the sound we're looking for, we can shape our vocal tract during inhalation. When we breathe in through the shape of the upcoming sound, we make sure that when the vocal folds begin to vibrate, the vocal tract is prepared, and the first sound that leaves our bodies is clean, precise, and ready to meet the emotional moment.

When the inhalation doesn't prepare the vocal tract, the singer has to find the right position on the fly. Sometimes that means that the first few tones don't quite match the rest of the phrase, as the singer finds their sweet spot just a few seconds too late. But beginning singers often find that rearranging their vocal tract mid-phrase is akin to changing direction in midair, and the whole phrase, or even the whole song, gets stuck in their default inhalatory position. Inhalation is, quite literally, an opportunity to set yourself up for success.

An essential part of this successful set up is avoiding any tension or effort in the inhalation. When the inhalation is easy and extraneous muscles are not recruited, the resonance of the following phrase is greater. In turn, when the resonance is greater, the muscles often remain released and relaxed, as the student comfortably relies on resonance rather than muscular effort to achieve their desired sound. Spending time on breathing may seem superfluous if your student's issue is one of resonance, but the right inhalation can start an upward spiral, and keep your student on the right track.

Resonance and Phonation

Recent research in voice science suggests that resonance isn't just the end product of the vocal system, but also part of what makes that system work.[44] Resonance both above and below the vocal folds can actually help the vocal folds vibrate freely and flexibly. So, aligning your vocal tract in a way that amplifies the sound makes it easier to produce that sound. A student who struggles with phonation issues, particularly hyperfunctional phonation issues, might benefit from focusing on resonance and allowing those vibrations to help them find ease in tone production.

Resonance and Support

We've often described resonance strategies to our students as ways to get more bang for your proverbial vocal buck. Remember that formants amplify frequencies within their range and attenuate those outside it. So properly aligning the formants with the pitch and its overtones will provide a major boost in volume. Drawing your student's attention to this fact can help alleviate excess subglottal pressure or pushing stemming from a desire to be louder. In this way, finding and maintaining solid resonance can help alleviate support issues.

Resonance and Registration

Have you ever noticed that it's difficult to belt an "ooh" sound? Or that "ee" doesn't work well in the top of the treble voice? Or that pop singers often sing "ay" instead of "ee" (think N'sync's "It's gonna be me")? Really nailing a specific timbre involves a complex interplay between resonance and registration, both because of the way registration affects spectral slope, and because of the way resonance influences phonation (as mentioned a few paragraphs ago). Formant configurations of vowels mean that some work better than others for each kind of sound.

---

[44] Lucero, Jorge C., Kélem G. Lourenço, Nicolas Hermant, Annemie Van Hirtum, and Xavier Pelorson. "Effect of source–tract acoustical coupling on the oscillation onset of the vocal folds." The Journal of the Acoustical Society of America 132, no. 1 (2012): 403-411.

Wade, Laura, Noel Hanna, John Smith, and Joe Wolfe. "The role of vocal tract and subglottal resonances in producing vocal instabilities." The Journal of the Acoustical Society of America 141, no. 3 (2017): 1546-1559.

For example, the belt sound is characterized by a strong second formant that lines up with the first harmonic, and a weaker fundamental frequency, which is made possible by the milder spectral slope of a TA dominant sound.

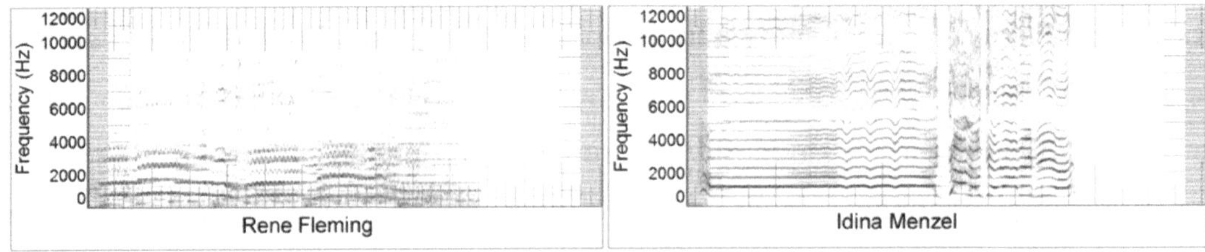

Figure 9.8 - Spectrogram of an operatic singer (Renee Fleming) compared with that of a belter (Idina Menzel)

Vowels with a back tongue position, like “oh” and “ooh” have a second formant that is too low to line up with the first harmonic for most pitches in the belt range. Closed vowels, like “ee” and “ooh” have a low first formant that can align too closely with the fundamental frequency, boosting it too much for a true belt timbre. So, belters love a good “ae” vowel, like in the word “yeah,” because it combines an open mouth position with a forward tongue. Figuring all of that out can be complicated, but following some general guidelines for vowels is simple:

1. Open vowels, like “ah,” encourage more chest voice. For belting, aim for open vowels and a forward tongue.
2. Closed and back vowels, like “ooh” and “oh” help encourage more head voice, and can be useful to encourage a legit sound or move to a headier mix.
3. Forward and closed vowels, like “ee” and “ay” are great for a chest mix because of the forward placement of the tongue.

Finding exactly the right vowel for a specific student and spot is always an experiment, but you can use these principles to guide your trials until you find the right option.

Introducing Belting

As we’ve previously stated, belting is a phenomenon of both registration and resonance. Achieving a healthy, effective belt sound requires implementing strategies from both areas of vocal technique. Consistently accessing both a flexible TA-dominant mix and twang resonance are prerequisites for this work. Once your student is ready, we recommend starting with the following sequence.

1. Joyful Shout: Pretend that you see a friend across the street and exclaim "I just won a million dollars!" It's not yelling, it's more of a "call." "Calling" is a more open, embodied vocal quality: a shout, but not a yell. You can use any short sentence that expresses joy and delight: "Congratulations!", "I love you!", or "We won!"
2. Add twang resonance: See the section earlier in the chapter on twang and utilize those exercises to discover this kind of resonance. Then add twang to the joyful shout. Try phrases with lots of "ae" (as in cat) vowels, like "Yeah, yeah, yeah!" or "That damn cat!" and keep the corners of the mouth wide.
3. Add pitch: You can make up pitches or use a melody line from the student's repertoire, but we recommend starting with either a descending line, or one that ascends and then descends. Ending on the highest note is often harder than moving through it. Be sure to use a physical gesture, such as throwing a ball away, to "release" the energy required for this very athletic vocal production. The belt sound should always feel like it's moving away from you. Stalled energy, or stuck energy, is not conducive to healthy belting, twangy or not.
4. Discover auxiliary support: The techniques for grounding we described in the previous chapter provide the final piece of this puzzle. These methods will take stress off the larynx by recruiting other muscles in the body. But be careful that this extra muscular work doesn't induce constriction in the larynx and vocal tract. Maintaining a sense of movement and flexibility is key.

This method is, of course, not the only effective way to teach belting, but it is the way in which we've had the most success. There's also much more to learn once this foundation has been established. Sustaining the belt sound for longer will require a stronger sense of support that must be conditioned. Carrying the belt higher will require more flexibility in the larynx, which is facilitated by a whining quality in the moment, and by the development of a robust head register throughout a singer's training. The high belt (above D_5) also requires more closed vowels like "ay" and "ee," due to shifts in formant frequencies in that range. But all these advances must be built on a solid foundation of flexible registration and efficient resonance.

Chapter 10: Articulation

The Science of Articulation

How do consonants influence our singing?

If you think of our air's pathway through our body as we sing, articulation is the last stage of the process, the final influence on our sound. Even though articulation sits at the end of our flowchart, its implications can affect the entire process of singing, and every other area of vocal technique. Producing consonants requires that we move the soft tissue of the vocal tract, which affects our formants and resonance. Articulatory muscles can affect the position of the larynx and the function of the intrinsic laryngeal muscles, which impacts registration and phonation. Certain consonants can encourage or discourage air flow, affecting our support. Tension in the articulatory muscles can inhibit our inhalation and alter the relaxed and ready state of our whole bodies. No wonder it's often harder to sing the full text, as opposed to just vowels or single syllables.

Although vowel and consonant formation should function as a unit, the muscular processes involved in consonant articulation must be considered distinct from those of vowel formation. Each vowel has a particular shape and resonance characteristic that requires a relatively fixed adjustment of the pharynx, so the voice is consistent in its resonance. Conversely, the muscles of the tongue, lips, jaw, and face must be highly flexible for the articulation of fast moving, ever-changing consonants. Vowels formed without constriction allow the tongue, lips, jaw, and facial muscles to move freely. The goal is for tone and articulation to become independent of each other. When this goal is achieved, the voice will emerge freely and easily, the tone quality will be pure, the articulation clear, and the text easily understandable.

What structures are we working with?

The Tongue

Perhaps the most important articulatory structure is the tongue: it is responsible not just for consonant production, but also our vowels. You're likely most aware of the blade of your tongue, also called the dorsum, but the tongue extends much farther back, down the throat to the hyoid bone.

This large structure is composed of four different groups of muscles. The superior longitudinal muscle runs along the top of the tongue, and when contracted alone, it curls the tip of the tongue upwards. The inferior longitudinal muscle mirrors the superior but on the bottom of the tongue; contracting it alone pulls the tip of the tongue down. Contracting together, these two muscles shorten the tongue. In between the superior and inferior longitudinal muscles are the horizontal and vertical tongue muscles. Contraction of the horizontal tongue muscles is what brings the sides of the tongue up. Contraction of the vertical muscles flattens the tongue.

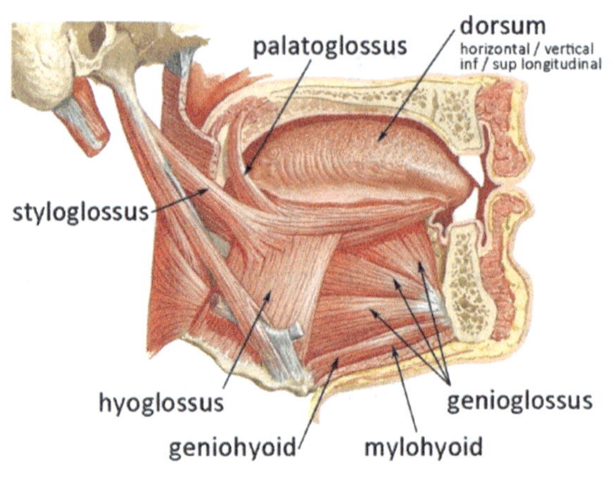

Figure 10.1 - Muscles of the tongue

Those intrinsic muscles shape the tongue itself, but the tongue's connections, via its extrinsic muscles, can shape the whole of the vocal tract. As you read about all these connections in this paragraph, try moving your tongue in all these ways and isolating the function of these muscles. The palatoglossus muscle runs from the soft palate, through the walls of the throat to the base of the tongue. When contracted, it can raise the back of the tongue and/or lower the soft palate. The styloglossus muscle originates at the styloid process and is also responsible for raising the back of the tongue. The hyoglossus muscle connects the tongue to the hyoid bone, and it is responsible for depressing and retracting the tongue. And, finally, the genioglossus connects the tongue to the chin and allows us to pull the tongue forward.

Tongue tension is a common problem among singers, and it's easy to see why: there are so many muscles to tense! It's possible for that tension to occur in the dorsum, where we have plenty of nerve endings. But it's more likely that tension will build up in the deeper parts of the tongue and its extrinsic muscles where we have fewer nerve endings, meaning it can be difficult to sense for beginning singers. The importance of the tongue in producing language and its connections to other major parts of the vocal tract means tension in the tongue is, unfortunately, a considerable obstacle in singing. We'll address strategies for relieving this tension further in the chapter.

The Palate

Put your tongue behind your upper teeth and start tracing backward along the roof of your mouth. The first structure you'll feel is the alveolar ridge, that bony ledge where your tongue lands when you form an "n" sound. Beyond that is the hard palate. The tip of your tongue should just barely reach your soft palate, the squishy part way in the back. As we discussed in the previous chapter, the soft palate raises to close off the nasal cavity and is a major determinant of our resonance. It's also a part of many consonant sounds, particularly the nasal consonants like "m," "n," and "ng" that require an open nasal cavity.

The levator palatini muscle pulls the soft palate up and back, while the tensor palatini muscle flattens the palate (this flattening assists in equalizing air pressure in the middle ear). Both of these muscles help form the soft palate itself and connect to the skull and the auditory tubes in the ear.[45] The palatoglossus, as mentioned above, and the palatopharyngeus—which originates in the soft palate and travels through the pharynx to insert into the thyroid cartilage—lower the soft palate. This connection to the thyroid cartilage means that movements of the soft palate can have a direct effect on laryngeal position. The soft palate is also subject to gravity, so if the levator and tensor palatini muscles are relaxed, the palate will passively depress. The same is true for lifting the soft palate if the singer is lying down or, in extreme cases, upside down.

---

[45] The musculus uvulae, the muscle in the uvula, can also be recruited to increase resonance space by further lifting the palate. When this muscle is contracted, the uvula will flatten out against the roof of the mouth. However, this extreme lift is rarely useful for musical theater singing and is more often applied in the classical genre.

As we mentioned in the previous chapter, the soft palate serves greater purposes in our human body, one of which is assisting in swallowing. When we swallow, the soft palate lifts to ensure that all our food moves toward the esophagus, rather than out our nose. The swallowing reflex also lifts the larynx. This pairing of functions through the swallowing process is unfortunate for singers. Take a guess at how many times you swallow in a day. Now multiply that out across your whole life. Every time you've ever swallowed, you've taught your body that lifting the soft palate and lifting the larynx go together. But the pursuit of clear articulation and resonance demands that we separate these two functions and learn how to manipulate our soft palate and our larynx. independently of each other.

The Jaw

As one of our singing teachers was fond of saying, "You could sing very well without a jaw." This suggestion is obviously not entirely true or practical, but the broader point here is that jaw movements are less imperative for articulation than we tend to think. In fact, excess muscular action in and around the jaw inhibits our ability to sing freely.

The muscles of the jaw are fundamentally imbalanced. The muscles that close the jaw—the masseter, internal pterygoid, and the temporalis—are very strong because they are anchored to the skull. Your masseter is easy to find: place your hands on your cheeks, closer to your ears than your mouth, and bite down; you'll feel it bulge under your fingers. The masseter and the internal pterygoid work together to form a sling-like structure that closes and retracts the jaw. Now find your temporalis: put your hands on the side of your head, above your ears, and bite down again. Contracting this muscle snaps your jaw closed.

There are three muscles responsible for opening the jaw: the digastric muscle, the mylohyoid, and the geniohyoid. These muscles are weaker than those that close the jaw because they are anchored to the movable hyoid bone, as opposed to the very stable skull. The digastric muscle has two bellies, and runs between the mastoid process, hyoid bone, and the mandible. It both opens the jaw and raises the larynx for swallowing. The mylohyoid forms the muscular floor of the mouth, and it runs from the mandible to the hyoid bone. Finally, the geniohyoid connects the chin to the hyoid bone (see figure 10.1).

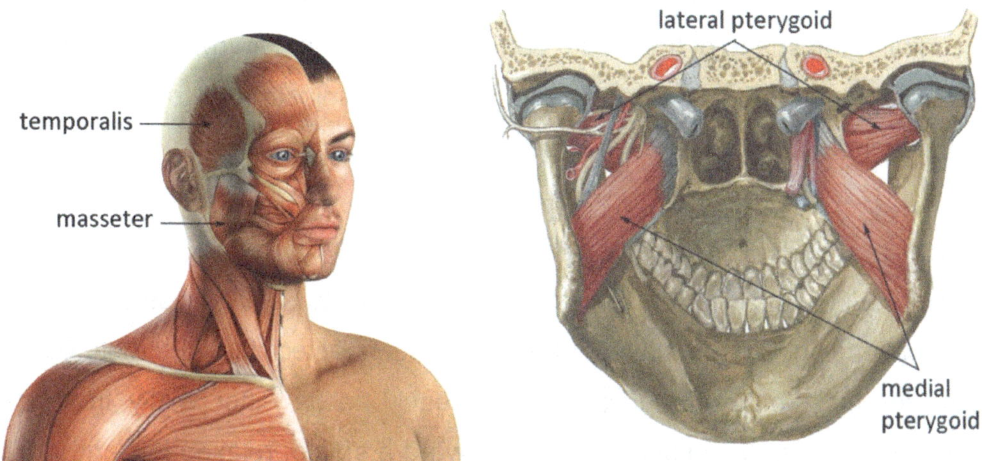

Figure 10.2 - Jaw elevators

Netter medical illustration (right image) used with permission of Elsevier.

Excess tension in the jaw is a problem because of the jaw muscles' connections to the hyoid bone. Instability in the jaw will therefore lead to an unstable laryngeal position. And because the two sets of muscles that control the jaw—those that open it and close it—are inherently out of balance, it's difficult to find stability in the jaw if these muscles are working against each other. Luckily, the jaw, like the rest of our bodies, is subject to gravity. A fully relaxed jaw will hang open, relieving the opening muscles of duty. Sometimes a more open position is required, particularly for belting and singing higher pitches, but that slightly open position works more often than you'd think. Further on in the chapter, we'll discuss strategies for finding and maintaining that position.

The Lips

Nine times out of ten, the first time a student achieves a truly relaxed position of the jaw, the clarity of their diction will suffer. It will feel, and sound, as if they've just come from the dentist and their mouth is full of Novocain. The issue here is not that the jaw is too relaxed, but rather that immobilizing the jaw has also immobilized the lips.

The good news about the lips is that their muscles are, for the most part, disconnected from the rest of our vocal mechanism. Most of the muscles that manipulate the lips attach to the skull or the cheekbones, meaning we can move our lips without affecting the position of other essential structures, like the hyoid bone or the tongue. This is not to say that the position of our lips doesn't influence our sound; on the contrary, the shape of the mouth partially determines our vowels and therefore a lot of our resonance. But it is possible to make such adjustments to the position of the lips independently of other vocal structures.

How do we articulate without messing everything up?

In short, we work toward independence of the articulatory muscles and structures. This work is challenging, first because of how interconnected these structures are. Secondly, for most of us Americans, our speech habits differ wildly from ideal articulation for singing. In singing, we strive toward a stable, relaxed jaw and a free, flexible, and active tongue. But observe just about anyone in speech and you'll see exactly the opposite: we tend to over-utilize the jaw and under-utilize the tongue, so that the tongue only moves in concert with the jaw. The first step toward free articulation is breaking that link; we'll discuss strategies for that further on in the chapter.

Maintaining independence of jaw and tongue, especially as you move through different repertoire, means producing each consonant sound with only the articulatory movements that are essential to that sound. For example, if you ask most people to say "na na na," you'll see their jaws move up and down with each "n" sound. But what creates that "n" sound is the tongue hitting the hard palate while air flows through the nose—no jaw movement is necessary! Try pronouncing an "n" sound with and without moving your jaw; you'll notice that once you've mastered that flipping up motion of the tongue, you can make that sound much more easily.

There are consonant charts, borrowed from our colleagues in the speech realm, that describe exactly where and how each consonant sound is formed, like this one (Figure 10.3):

These charts can be complicated and feature lots of jargon, but you don't have to start there. You can begin this exploration simply by moving through the alphabet, or speaking a phrase from a song, and keeping your jaw as still and relaxed as possible. You'll notice the jaw has to move for certain sounds, like "s" or "j" as in "judge." But you'll find that for other sounds, like "g" as in "goal" or "l" as in "lake," your tongue can do all the work.[46]

Classification of NAE Consonant Phonemes							
Manner of Articulation	**Place of Articulation**						
	Bilabial	**Labiodental**	**Dental**	**Alveolar**	**Palatal**	**Velar**	**Glottal**
Stop **Voiceless** **Voiced**	p b			t d		k g	
Fricative **Voiceless** **Voiced**		f v	θ ð	s z	ʃ ʒ		h
Affricate **Voiceless** **Voiced**					tʃ dʒ		
Nasal **Voiced**	m			n		ŋ	
Liquid **Voiced**				l	r		
Glide **Voiced**	w				y		

Figure 10.3 - North American English consonant chart[47]

The Art of Articulation

The story must be clear. The diction should not call attention to itself. It should seem organic and truthful. – Mary Saunders Barton[48]

Words, and more specifically consonants, are what separate the voice from other instruments: they put the "theater" in "musical theater." As we've said repeatedly, in musical theater, the words come first. The singer's first priority must be to establish a detailed understanding of the contents of the text. A crucial first step is to take the text away from the music. Reciting the text as a monologue gives the singer the opportunity to observe their natural inflection, take note of punctuation, and determine which words need emphasis. Taking this understanding back to the music often reveals something

[46] The classical vocal pedagogue William Vennard is known for his work with articulation. His book, *Singing: the Mechanism and the Technic*, provides thorough descriptions of the production of every consonant sound. However, his work is based firmly on classical singing technique, so it is not always applicable to musical theater work.

[47] Yoshida, Maria. "Consonant & Vowel Charts: North American English." Teaching Pronunciation Skills. https://teachingpronunciation.weebly.com/consonant--vowel-charts-nae.html.

[48] Benson, Elizabeth Ann. *Training Contemporary Commercial Singers.* Routledge, 2015: 172.

about the song's construction. The phrasing of most musical theater songs is based on the meaning of the sentence, so that the rhythm and melody both reflect and highlight the emotional intention. Beyond this dramatic work (and the technical work of finding articulatory independence that we'll discuss later in the chapter), the various vocal styles of the musical theater genre greatly affect articulation.

Traditional Legit

The traditional legit style relies on a warm, rounded tone. Crisp, quick consonants keep the text clear while not compromising the quality of the vowels. While the text should still maintain some colloquialism, the diction in this style will be the farthest removed from normal speech because the integrity of the vowel must be maintained.

Belt

The traditional belt is closer to calling than talking. Think about the difference between saying "Hey there," to someone passing you in the hallway, and calling out "Hey there!" to your neighbor across the street. In belting, consonants often shift to accommodate this more open position. But belting is still grounded in speech, so only minimal adjustments are used to maintain the belt timbre.

Contemporary

The mixed belt often used in the contemporary styles requires chattier articulation. This style of articulation will likely be the closest to regular speech, but more energized and enunciated so it is clear on stage. The jaw, tongue, and lips will all need to be more active, so it's imperative that they are free from tension.

Pop/Rock

In rock or pop influenced shows, the percussiveness of the text is often part of the rhythmic fabric of the music, so the diction should be crunchy to fill its place in the texture. This style often goes beyond what would be normal in conversation by over-emphasizing certain consonants, or adding shadow vowels for emphasis, like "you-uh" or "you don't know-uh."

Matching the Emotion

Of course, the emotional content of each moment must be a consideration. Try saying the phrase "get out of here," first like you're joking around with a friend, then like you're expressing incredulity, then one more time as if you're angry. How did your articulation change? Did you notice that you emphasized, or even dropped, different consonants? Did you notice your jaw and tongue reacting to the changes in your expression? Our emotions clearly influence the way we articulate in speech, so the same must be true for our singing if it is to be "organic and truthful."

The Art of Teaching Articulation

> *The percussive element in the lyric often provides an essential part of the rhythmic fabric of the song. The primary articulators—the tongue and lips—need coordination work as a routine part of a practice regiment in order to achieve percussive 'tightness' in a similar way to drummers and percussionists who use their hands"* – Kim Chandler[50]

How can you talk to your students about articulation?

We hope we have convinced you that working on articulation entails more than clarifying a singer's diction. It's important to help your students understand this idea, too. Focusing on the construction and execution of each individual consonant in a phrase can feel tedious, even superfluous. Disconnecting that work from its broader technical implications can leave a singer with constricted, unnatural diction. Divorcing that work from its dramatic influences creates a performance that is intelligible but lacks emotional depth or clarity. And, for the student, articulation work in a vacuum can feel pointlessly discouraging.

Diction work in which we just prod our students to enunciate implies an assumption of articulatory laziness on the part of the singer. Be careful of making that assumption, as it can mask a deeper issue—like tongue or jaw tension—that is preventing the singer from articulating clearly. To make matters worse, the singer suffering from excess tension will often try harder and introduce more constriction when prodded to

---

[50] Benson, Elizabeth Ann. *Training Contemporary Commercial Singers.* Compton Publishing, 2020: 169.

enunciate. It's an avoidable vicious cycle, provided we remember how deeply connected articulation is to the whole of our students' singing.

We recommend approaching articulation not as a collection of problems to be fixed, but as a gateway to more functional, more expressive singing. Sure, a rogue "L" is often a wrench in the gears, but a well-placed "g" is an incredible boon! Help your students become adept not just at recognizing and fixing problems in their articulation, but also at identifying opportunities, both technical and dramatic, that consonants can present. Our experience is that this approach energizes articulatory work for students and teachers alike.

What techniques and exercises are useful?

Exercises for articulatory independence

The first goal of articulation work is for tone and articulation to become independent of each other. If the tongue, lips, and jaw can move independently of the rest of the vocal mechanism, both the tone and the diction will be clear. These exercises are meant to encourage free functioning of the articulatory anatomy.

➢ Consonants with Vowels as Leaders

Speak a full, connected, resonant, "uh," elongating the vowel into a drone. Drop in an "m" so that you have "uh-muh-muh-muh." The consonant should be quick and late so that the vowel shape and resonance are not compromised. Now try "uh-duh-duh-duh," and "uh-luh-luh-luh." Reverse the order and pronounce the consonant first, then the vowel: "duh-duh-duh," "luh, luh, luh," and "muh, muh, muh." These exercises should be accomplished without moving the jaw.

➢ Tongue Twisters

All consonants in their different ways stop, diminish, or change the quality of resonance in the voice. The goal is to pronounce them so the text is clear and the flow of resonance is unimpeded, which requires considerable agility in the lips, tongue, and soft palate. Tongue twisters are very useful for this purpose if they are practiced carefully. Be sure the tongue is flexible and free (without pushing downward), the jaw has freedom to move, and the teeth stay apart as much as possible.

We've provided a few useful tongue twisters here that involve different types of consonants. These can be spoken or turned into vocal exercises.

- Messy Manny Makes Many Mudpies
- My Mom's Become a Brand-New Nun
- The Buzzing beneath the Bed is Bernard
- Velvety Violet Vacillates Vividly in Velvet and Velour
- Zsa Zsa Usually Uses Beige in her Unusual Montages
- Robert Rarely Remembers Rare Red Roses
- Five Firefighters Found the Fearful Feline Freaking Out
- Six Thick Thistle Sticks
- Lonely Larry Left London Long Ago

- Tongue Out / Tongue In

  Have the singer sing the text with the tongue resting on the bottom lip, making sure that each word is intelligible. Then ask the singer to sing the words with the tongue in its normal position, just behind the bottom teeth.

- Palatal awareness and independence exercises

  The beginning stages of sneezes, yawns, and swallows all involve a lift in the soft palate. Prompting your student to explore just the beginning sensations of these functions may help them feel their soft palate move.

Exercises for articulation and expression

The ultimate goal of articulation work is to help the student articulate the text in a way that is not only free, but also expressive. These exercises are intended to help the singer relate pronunciation to emotion and meaning, letting their feelings about the words guide their articulation.

- Words and Images

  Think of a word with a representational picture (examples: airplane, butterfly, waves, stream, blaze, sparks etc.). Close your eyes, and in your mind's eye, see the picture clearly. Allow your feelings to respond to the image. Then, speak the word with and through whatever feelings arose in your mind. Try different words that bring up different emotions and notice how your articulation changes.

➢ Words and Abstract Images

Think of a word with an abstract image (examples: love, rage, giggle, orange, pink, black, etc.). You may find that the meaning makes direct contact with your feelings, or that the abstract images grow out of what the word means to you. Let the feelings flow back through the word and express it.

What pitfalls should I watch out for?

Problems related to articulation generally fall into one of two categories: hypofunctional use of the lips, jaw, or tongue, or hyperfunctional use of the lips, jaw, or tongue. Hypofunctional use of the articulators is the less common of the two and can be easily corrected by asking for exaggerated movement of the lips, jaw, and facial muscles. Reconnecting to the narrative and dramatic intention of the song can help as well, as we naturally engage our articulatory anatomy more when we are emotionally invested in what we're communicating.

Hyperfunctional use of the articulators is very common. This issue is caused by excess tension: the lips can be locked and rigid; the jaw can be pushed down, out, or clenched; and the tongue might be pulled back or held elevated in the mouth. These issues result in garbled, strenuous diction that clouds and distorts the tone. The first step in solving this problem is to find relaxation in the whole body, and then specifically in the articulators. General stretching and breathing exercises are a great start, followed by yawn-sighs to stretch and relax the face specifically. Massaging the jaw and tongue muscles can also be helpful.

Once relaxation is achieved, start working toward free movement of the articulatory anatomy. Work for tongue agility with exercises using dental and alveolar consonants. Extend the tongue outside of the mouth and do circles clockwise and counterclockwise. Ask the student to hum, chew, and paint the inside of the mouth with the tongue simultaneously. The end goal is a stable and relaxed jaw, a free and flexible tongue, and active and mobile lips.

Finally, there are a few consonants in the English language that present specific challenges. American English speakers generally pronounce "L" sounds by pressing down the back of the tongue. In singing, however, the "L" sound should be produced only by moving the front of the tongue; this method doesn't displace the tongue or affect laryngeal position. The American, or rhotic, "r" also pulls the tongue back and, unless produced carefully, can influence any preceding vowels. Anticipating an "ng" sound may cause the palate to drop, as the singer prepares too early to produce that nasal sound. Watch out for these sounds in your students' repertoire; they can be a wrench in the gears.

Articulation and the Flowchart

Alignment > Breathing > Phonation > Support > Registration > Resonance > Articulation

Articulation and Alignment

> *The science of alignment is that when things are aligned, all coordinations are possible. Breathing, range, resonance, articulation, and connection, are all by-products of this…Stability and balance from the feet up is essential, with no extraneous work going on from the jaw or the neck.* – Amanda Colliver[51]

Overall posture and head position significantly influence jaw and tongue tension. Poor alignment also affects the constrictor muscles in the neck and throat. If your student is struggling with articulatory freedom, observe their alignment, specifically the way the head is positioned atop the spine. If the head is well balanced, no excess muscular work in the neck is required, and the constrictor muscles and muscles of the jaw can remain free.

---

[51] Melton, Joan. Singing in musical theatre: The training of singers and actors. Simon and Schuster, 2010: 175.

Articulation and Breathing

The ideal time to think about freedom in the articulatory anatomy is during inhalation. If a singer can learn to inhale through a relaxed articulatory structure, it's much more likely that the singing that follows will maintain that relaxation. Even if it doesn't, incorporating articulatory freedom into each inhalation means that every breath is a new chance to release tension. Unfortunately, many beginning singers habitually inhale with the muscles of the pharynx tightened, which results in a noisy inhalation. Sometimes, in the attempt to "make space," they over-engage the muscles of the vocal tract, making it impossible to bring the jaw and tongue into a neutral, relaxed position. In this case, a return to the basics of inhalation may be helpful. Refocusing on a relaxed and expansive breath often relieves tension in the vocal tract.

Articulation and Phonation

The tongue's connection to the hyoid bone means it has a direct impact on the position and function of the larynx. If the back of the tongue pushes down on the larynx, the valving action of the larynx—allowing the correct amount of breath to flow through consistently—cannot work correctly. If the articulators are tight, the tone very often will be tight as well. For this reason, it can be beneficial to introduce exercises that free up the articulators, particularly the tongue, early in a singer's training, especially if the tone is pressed or the singer experiences tightness or discomfort while they're singing.

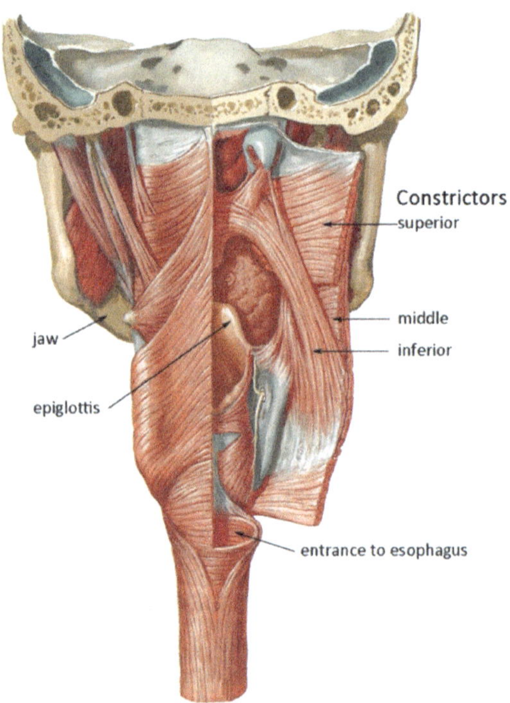

Figure 10.4 - Pharyngeal constrictors

Netter medical illustration used with permission of Elsevier.

Articulation and Support

The mouth, just like the larynx, functions as a valve for air. The actions of the mouth affect the air pressure behind it, and therefore affect the function of the vocal folds. During vowel production, when the mouth is open, the vocal folds alone hold back the air flow. But consonants, especially fricatives and plosives like f's or p's, affect airflow, and therefore affect support. Voiced fricatives, like v's and voiced th sounds (as in the word "that"), can be particularly effective for training support, as they help hold back some air, and can make it easier for a student to maintain expansion as they sing through a phrase. Plosives, on the other hand, often come with a big puff of air. Too much air being released at once can erode a singer's support for the rest of the phrase, so plosives must be treated with care—they should release as little air as possible while still being intelligible. Singing directly in front of a lit candle will reveal any large puffs of air as the flame flickers, or worse, goes out.

Articulation and Registration

The tongue's connections to the hyoid bone make tongue position and tongue tension extremely relevant to registration. Tension in the tongue can depress or elevate the larynx, both of which can result in the inability to regulate registration. Artificially depressing the larynx, is particularly antithetical to belting, so dealing with tongue tension is often a vital part of belting work. Over elevation of the larynx is an issue too, as it restricts the tilt of the thyroid cartilage and prevents the vocal folds from elongating. If the tongue is the true culprit in a student's registration issues, reach for exercises that use g's and k's: as long as these sounds are produced without moving the jaw, they force the back of the tongue to release.

Articulation and Resonance

Articulation inherently changes the shape of the vocal tract, so it has a strong influence on the consistency of resonance. Crisp, quick consonants produced without extraneous movement allow for the most consistent resonance. Most American English speakers, however, like to "chew their words" and over involve the jaw in articulation. Keeping the jaw slightly open and relaxed as much as possible is ideal. To find this position, imagine you've just been to the dentist and had a lot of novacaine.

Or alternately stretch and close the jaw a few times, and then see if you can arrive at a neutral position in the middle. Some pitches and/or registration events require a more open jaw position, and some consonants will require you to close the jaw. But more often than not, this position is feasible, and sticking to it will help maintain consistent, clear resonance.

Chapter 11: Final Points

We titled this book *Musical Theater Vocal Pedagogy: The Art and Science* because it sums up our philosophy on teaching musical theater voice. We, as voice teachers, live at the intersection of art—self-expression, nuance, and emotion—and science—calculation, experimentation, and precision. We hope that after reading this book, you feel more comfortable toggling between these two modes of thinking, and even blurring the lines, as you and your student chart their vocal and artistic wildernesses together. In this final chapter, we'll discuss a few elements of the science, the art, and the art of teaching that we have yet to address in previous chapters, but that are no less consequential to our work.

The Science

Vocal Health

We've said throughout this book that musical theater allows for any and all sounds in the service of expression. Unfortunately, that can include unhealthy sounds. In our experience, the incidence of vocal injury in musical theater singers is higher than in classical singers. The style of the music, and the visceral emotion involved, make it more difficult to evaluate the balance between what is a resonant and exciting sound produced healthily and what is the result of constriction. Furthermore, professional musical theater singers are expected to perform eight shows a week, which is an incredible amount of voice use, even with the benefits of amplification and a perfectly healthy technique.

As musical theater singers get closer and closer to professional careers, they must be more and more vigilant about their own vocal health. The industry is not designed to protect their voices; they must be their own advocates. Teaching your singers to be mindful of their vocal health, to know when to seek help, and how to advocate for their needs is paramount in making sure their career is not only successful, but also sustainable.

Vocal health is a concern for teachers as well. Teachers spend an incredible amount of time talking each day. Even for non-singers, that much voice use warrants special care. Here are some general dos and don'ts to be mindful of as you and your students work to keep your voices healthy:

Dos:

- Get enough rest. Prioritize sleep and leisure as much as you can and try to take one day off from voice work per week.
- Adopt good posture and alignment habits throughout your daily life.
- Be mindful of your vocal technique throughout your daily life, particularly when speaking for long periods of time.
- Stay well hydrated (laryngologists remind us to "sing wet, pee pale".
- Maintain a humid living environment (40-50 percent humidity).
- Wash your hands frequently.
- Take time to recover from illness; rest your voice with your body.
- Recognize when your voice is strained. Consult a physician if you experience throat symptoms or voice change for more than ten days.

Don'ts:

- Don't inhale harmful substances such as tobacco and recreational drugs.
- Avoid alcohol, especially before voice use.
- Avoid any foods or behaviors that cause acid reflux.
- Don't speak too much or too loudly, especially in noisy environments.
- Avoid screaming and yelling.
- Avoid clearing your throat as much as you can; instead, yawn, drink water, or hum gently.
- Don't overuse over-the-counter preparations for colds and allergies, especially antihistamines and ibuprofen.
- Don't sing beyond your comfortable range (know your physical limits for pitch and loudness).
- Don't talk with a low-pitched monotone voice; keep your voice powered by breath flow so the tone carries and varies.

Under normal circumstances, the larynx is very tough and usually requires only proper rest, good nutrition, and thorough hydration. But particularly for professional voice users, vocal health is not something to be taken lightly. Pathologic disorders can result from sustained abuse/overuse of the voice, trauma, or medical illness. If you notice any of the following symptoms in yourself or your students, we recommend consulting an otolaryngologist (ENT):[52]

- Changes in the voice or hoarseness that persist more than 2 weeks.
- Sudden loss of voice or other change, especially during a performance or voice use.
- Consistent, unresolved breathiness.
- Pain with voice use.
- Something just doesn't feel right.

While it may be cost prohibitive, it is advisable that singers get an annual exam from a laryngologist, even when they feel healthy. Ideally, singers should see an ENT for preventative reasons, to establish a relationship before any problems arise. An ENT can help singers identify issues that may put them at risk for vocal injury, discuss mild symptoms they might be overlooking, and learn more about their own instruments so they can be more aware of any future issues.

Extended Vocal Techniques

Some genres of contemporary commercial music call for extended vocal techniques that sound rough or harsh but ***can*** be produced healthily. Particularly in the rock genre, singers often growl, scream, grunt, or creak. As the musical theater industry becomes more and more entwined with other commercial music genres, it becomes important for musical theater singers to learn to reproduce these effects. Singers often learn these techniques through imitation, but that can unfortunately lead to unhealthy constriction as singers struggle to match what they hear by any means necessary. But understanding the anatomy and physiology of the voice means that you can help them

---

[52] An ENT, or an Ear, Nose, and Throat doctor, is also called an otolaryngologist. A laryngologist is an ENT who subspecializes in laryngology, so they deal with the voice specifically. For singers and other professional voice users, a board-certified laryngologist is the best choice.

achieve these sounds in a healthy way, free from unnecessary force or constriction. We've provided a list of some of these techniques in the Appendix (page 136), along with an explanation of the physiological function behind them and exercises that help encourage that function.

Learning More

We've introduced voice science, but if you're intrigued, there's much more to learn! The *Journal of Singing* and The *Journal of Voice* are excellent resources for new research. We, as a field, are learning new things all the time, and musical theater vocal pedagogy is a growing area of interest for many voice researchers. Staying current with these publications will keep you up to date with voice science as we continue to understand more and more about the human voice.

In addition to our own experience and expertise, we relied on a few books by other voice teachers to broaden our perspective. If you're looking to keep reading, we highly recommend the following books:

- *Training Contemporary Commercial Singers*, by Elizabeth Benson
- *Singing and the Actor*, by Gillyanne Kayes
- *Cross-Training in the Voice Studio*, by Norman Spivey and Mary Saunders Barton

The Art

Industry Concerns

The way the musical theater industry is structured, at least in its current iteration, presents additional challenges for singers beyond the basic issues of gaining functional vocal technique and learning how to express themselves. The musical theater industry is fiercely competitive; there are increasingly more performers vying for fewer jobs. Success requires incredible versatility; along with being a skilled actor, singer, and dancer, the aspiring performer must cultivate an acute awareness of the many different styles encompassed by the genre, so that they are prepared to audition for any and every opportunity. In the face of these incredible demands, it can be tempting to deprioritize technical work in favor of repertoire preparation, and simply troubleshoot technical issues as they arise. But stylistic fluency only functions in conjunction with a flexible and sustainable vocal technique. Building solid vocal technique must be our first concern if our singers are to adapt to this industry's demands.

The traditional typecasting of the industry presents another complication for training. Although there is a new wave of musical theater writing evolving—as in shows like *A Strange Loop*—in which writers are eschewing the traditional types in favor of greater authenticity, categories like "Leading Man," or "Character Actor" are still widely used. These labels are often based more on a singer's appearance than their vocal identity. Not knowing or playing toward their type may cost singers valuable opportunities, but boxing them into a type may limit their potential, especially if it is at odds with their vocal identity or personal style. Be aware too that the experience of objectification—being valued for your body and/or appearance rather than as a full person—is linked to negative mental health outcomes, like depression and eating disorders.[53] You may not be able to control the way your student is treated by the outside world, but in your studio, make sure they are seen as a whole person, not defined or limited by their appearance. You can fully acknowledge the injustices of the industry, be supportive as they step outside of their "type," and help them craft performances that more authentically reveal who they are.

Finally, and perhaps most distressingly, we have very little time to accomplish all these goals. Typically, aspiring musical theater performers need to be fully prepared by the time they reach their mid-twenties. We work with several excellent singing actors working regularly on Broadway who are in their early thirties and are no longer being called to audition for typical leading roles, but are instead playing parents, teachers, and other older supporting roles. Our work as voice trainers, therefore, must be efficient, succinct, and organized, to ensure the students gain all the information and skills they need in the shortest possible amount of time. Of course, none of this happens without the contributions of the student. The one absolutely essential ingredient for career success in this genre is discipline.

---

[53] Fredrickson, Barbara L., and Tomi-Ann Roberts. "Objectification theory: Toward understanding women's lived experiences and mental health risks." Psychology of women quarterly 21, no. 2 (1997): 173-206.

The American educational system in which a student enters college at age 18 and graduates at 22 was not designed with potential musical theater performers in mind, but there are several very successful undergraduate degree programs that consistently produce successful alumni. We believe that, although always imperfect, a bachelor's degree program is the most efficient way to gain skills and make effective connections, provided that program is designed to cater to industry demands and staffed with experienced and knowledgeable faculty.

The topic of how best to prepare future musical theater performers is controversial, and many in the field would disagree with our assertion that a bachelor's degree program is the best way. College programs are inherently flawed and certainly don't provide an ideal experience—particularly when you consider the cost of these institutions. However, we find that the alternative—taking private singing, dance, and acting lessons—relies heavily on a student's ability to identify the right teachers and programs, which is difficult to do without significant connections and resources. Good college programs are much easier to identify, and they package these experiences together. They can also offer scholarships and loans. Furthermore, a bachelor's degree provides somewhat of a safety net through greater access to other employment opportunities, although that is by no means guaranteed. Still, college is not the right choice for every student, and there are other ways to pursue a career in musical theater.

But be wary when evaluating collegiate programs: many schools have a musical theater program because these programs are often profitable, but few are actually up to the task of preparing working professionals consistently. We advise considering the following questions for students looking to choose a collegiate musical theater program:

- What is the musical theater program's overall reputation? Will this program provide me with useful connections and networking opportunities?
- How does the required curriculum compare to those of other top musical theater programs? How much of the required curriculum is relevant to my degree?

- ➢ How experienced are the faculty? Keep both industry and teaching experience in mind: just because someone is an accomplished performer doesn't mean they can teach well.
- ➢ Where are the school's alumni? How many have achieved my career goals?

We also advise talking with alumni and current students who can provide perspective on things like selecting classes, valuable opportunities the program provides, and, perhaps most importantly, which teachers to seek out. Even within the best programs in the country, there's no guarantee that a student's assigned voice teacher will be the best teacher for them. Although it may be cost prohibitive, we recommend taking sample lessons if at all possible. If sample lessons are not possible, you can rely on feedback from current students and alumni to determine different teachers' styles and effectiveness.

The Art of Teaching

Teacher Individuality

We've talked a lot in this book about the individuality of each student. What we haven't yet addressed is the individuality of each *teacher*. Your talents, personality, and creativity are an inevitable part of the teaching decisions you make, and that is as it should be! We are all better teachers when we bring our whole selves to the work. Your style of teaching is and should be different than anyone else's. As we stated in the introduction, our aim was not to provide exhaustive lists of exercises, but rather a few key vocalizes in each chapter that illustrate the principles of both science and style in that area. We chose this approach because it allows you to adapt to your students and your own style. Singing, particularly in this genre, must be a creative endeavor, and so should teaching it!

There are, however, some common principles we think are important to consider as you think about and cultivate your personal teaching style:

1. Keep up with the trends: go to the shows, read new books and articles, and listen to all kinds of music. Imitate the new sounds you hear and know how they're made in your own awareness.

2. Experiment! Be open to trying new repertoire, exercises, and techniques. Taking chances in your singing and teaching provides an excellent model for your students, and it keeps you connected to the learning process.
3. Forge a personal connection with your students. Within what is appropriate, share your stories of growth, exploration, courage, and even failure. Doing so builds trust and rapport between you and your student, which makes all their learning possible.

The realms of science and art can feel diametrically opposed, but they have at least one thing in common: exploration! Both mediums of thought are vehicles for exploration of our world and ourselves. We hope this book has invited you to joyfully, curiously, explore singing and teaching through scientific and artistic lenses. Even though you've finished reading, we hope you'll keep exploring.

Appendix

Rough Vocal Effects in Singing

Vocal effects are advanced singing techniques, and therefore they should only be attempted once a base level of healthy technique has been established. That healthy technique must include easy access to multiple modes of phonation, as these modes (such as head voice singing, chest voice, or belt) often provide the basis for the effect. These effects should not cause discomfort or pain, even when they are first attempted.

The vocal effects can be made at various levels of the vocal tract, and it is crucial to understand where the effort/work should be in the vocal tract to prevent injury. Effects can be made by:

- Vocal folds
- Ventricular/False folds
- Arytenoid cartilages, epiglottis, and aryepiglottic folds
- Piriform fossa and posterior pharyngeal wall of the hypopharynx
- Soft palate, uvula, back wall of the throat (oropharynx), and the back of the tongue
- The rest of the oral and nasal cavity

Keep in mind also that a microphone is imperative for many of these effects, both to allow the effect to sound to its full potential and to protect the singer from producing these sounds with too much intensity.[54]

Growl

Growl is created at the second level of the vocal tract, not at the vocal fold level. One of the methods for making this sound is by tipping the epiglottis over and allowing the arytenoids to hit the epiglottis in a drumming motion. Another method of creating this sound is by closing the epiglottis with the back of the tongue; this method may be more

[54] For more information on rough vocal effects, including examples, we recommend reviewing The Complete Vocal Technique research website at cvtresearch.com.

straightforward for those with no experience in making vocal effects. This sound is typical in jazz, R&B, and gospel music and can be used with all vocal modes.

Exercises to Find the Growl

- ➢ Method 1: At the level of the epiglottis and arytenoids
  - Close your mouth and clear your throat. Notice the brief rolling effect. Slowly extend that rolling effect but be careful not to force air out.
  - Once you can find the rolling effect and sustain it, open your mouth and continue that roll.
  - If this effect is uncomfortable, check the position of the larynx to make sure it is neutral, not too low.
- ➢ Method 2: Use the back of the tongue
  - Imitate Kermit the Frog.
  - Use twang to increase ease.

Distortion

When this technique is done correctly, the ventricular folds vibrate closely or directly touch one another, creating a mix of noise and tone. The true vocal folds below should not be affected by the vibration of the false folds above them and will generally vibrate double or triple the speed of the false folds. This technique requires a microphone.

Exercises to Find Distortion

- ➢ Method 1: Saying "aaa-eee"
  - Say "aaa-eee" in almost a whispering, mean voice.
  - Gradually extend the time making this noise.
  - Add pitch and repeat "aaa-eee" several times in a row quickly.
  - In this method, it is easier to find distortion in the singer's higher voice because the larynx is raised.
- ➢ Method 2: Saying "eh" with twang
  - Say "eh" (as in bet) with a twang quality.
  - Pulsate the sound and make it sound almost like a duck.

Rattle

Rattle is like distortion in its rolling sound, but it is much milder and less mean sounding. The arytenoids touch and hit each other, which is the secondary source of vibration that creates the vocal effect.

Exercise to Find Rattle

- Method: Imitating Crow Noises
  - Sigh on an "ah" in falsetto
  - Imitate a crow in the falsetto

Creak/Creaking

A creak and creaking are created at the vocal folds, so it is vital to be more cautious when making this effect. These effects are similar to vocal fry; using vocal fry can be an excellent jumping-off point for finding these vocal effects. Creak is an effect on the onset and offset of a phrase that follows or is followed by a clear note. Creaking is that same effect held along the length of the note. Creaking requires a microphone, as too much intensity behind this sound could be damaging.

Exercises to Find Creak

- Method for Finding Creak: Vocal Fry and Imitating a "Lazy" sound
  - Find the creak by starting in vocal fry; pretend to be "lazy" with your sound.
  - Transition from that fry sound to a sung phrase.
- Method for Sustaining Creak:
  - Call out "hey!" loudly and with lots of energy.
  - Then call out hey, with the same amount of energy, but in that "lazy," vocal fry-like way.

Fry Scream & Screaming

The fry scream builds off creaking and is therefore also produced at the level of the vocal folds.

Exercise to Find the Fry Scream:

- Method: Extending the creak
    - Start with a creak and gradually extend the length of that sound.
    - Then try the noise in your falsetto, while holding back volume.

Grunt

A grunt is mainly used in heavy metal music; the effect is dark, demonizing, loud, and noisy. This effect is produced throughout the vocal tract by the vocal folds, ventricular folds, epiglottis and arytenoids, the piriform fossa and posterior pharyngeal wall of the hypopharynx, and the soft palate, uvula, back wall of the throat (oropharynx) and the back of the tongue. It may be helpful to think that this sound combines the distortion and growl effects, and it is often paired with distortion to make this vocal effect sound meaner. This effect requires a microphone.

Exercise to Find the Grunt

- Method: Annoyed Grunts
    - Make annoyed grunting sounds in your falsetto.
    - With this grunting noise, pretend to bark like a dog.

About the Authors

Christopher Arneson is a professional voice trainer and vocologist on faculty at Westminster Choir College where he is Director of Voice Pedagogy, and at Princeton University. Dr. Arneson was the co-director of the Voice and Speech department in the MFA program at the renowned Actors Studio Drama School - New School University. He is the editor/author of *Fundamentals of Great Singing, the Teaching of Michael Trimble* and *Literature for Teaching: Solo Vocal Repertoire from a Developmental Perspective,* both from Inside View Press. Dr. Arneson is a member of the National Association of Teachers of Singing and the American Academy of Teachers of Singing.

Kirsten Shippert Brown is a vocal pedagogue, voice researcher, and singer currently on the faculty at Sarah Lawrence College and Iona University. Dr. Brown holds a Bachelor's degree in Voice and a Master of Business Administration degree from Stetson University, a Master's degree in Voice Pedagogy and Performance from Westminster Choir College, and a Doctorate of Education in the College Teaching of Music from Teachers College, Columbia University.

Index

A

B

C

D

E

F

G

M

N

O

P

Q

R

S

T

V

W

Y